UNDER
LIVE
OAKS

The Last Great Houses of the Old South

CAROLINE SEEBOHM
& PETER WOLOSZYNSKI

CLARKSON POTTER / PUBLISHERS
NEW YORK

Published by Clarkson Potter/Publishers, New York, New York. Member
of the Crown Publishing Group, a division of Random House, Inc.
www.randomhouse.com

CLARKSON N. POTTER is a trademark and POTTER and colophon
are registered trademarks of Random House, Inc.

Printed in China

Design by Donna Agajanian

PAGES 1, 2, AND 3:
*The meaning of the past,
memorialized on tabletops, in
glass cabinets, or glimpsed
through the shadows of a
window, remains alive in every
corner of these great houses
of the Old South.*
FRONTIS: *The graceful mansions
and lush gardens of the
Deep South, while serving as
reminders of a world long gone,
also demonstrate the power
of architecture and the natural
landscape to outlast history.*

Library of Congress Cataloging-in-Publication Data
Seebohm, Caroline.
    Under live oaks : the last great houses of the Old South / text by
Caroline Seebohm; photographs by Peter Woloszynski.
    1. Plantations—Southern States.   2. Architecture, Domestic—Southern
States—19th century.   3. Plantation life—Southern States—History.
I. Title.
NA7211 .S44   2002
728.8'0975'09034—dc21   2001059318

ISBN 0-609-60699-9

10 9 8 7 6 5 4 3 2 1

First Edition

Southerners tend to live in one place, where they can see whole lives unfold around them. It gives them a natural sense of the narrative, of the dramatic content of life.

—EUDORA WELTY

Contents

PREFACE

The first morning I woke up in America, in November 1991, was in Charleston, South Carolina. I was staying near the Battery, with a view of Fort Sumter. I thought Charleston was the most magnificent town I'd seen in years, and it was the inspiration for my subsequent journey through the South.

I believe that the only way to travel is to get lost. This approach was very helpful in discovering the South. Armed with only my Hasselblad camera, a tattered Rand McNally map, and the pure wonder of a boy turning over rocks, I drove through the most remote parts of the antebellum South, from Virginia to Georgia, from Mississippi to Louisiana, from Florida to Alabama, finding houses that took my breath away and people whose kindness overwhelmed me. They invited me to their most private lives, where only close relatives and friends had been before.

I returned home with a treasure trove of impressions and family histories and more than five hundred photographs that I was able to take during my extraordinary exploration. It is these pictures along with Caroline Seebohm's text that now form the content of this book.

—PETER WOLOSZYNSKI

An heirloom maple tester bed, antique lace, period wallpaper, personal portraits, and samplers bear witness to a family's history.

INTRODUCTION

What accounts for the enduring allure of the American South? This place is an unending source of fascination for many. Its traditions seem so appealing, yet its history is so fraught. Its trees and flowers are fragrant, yet its plantations of cotton and tobacco reek of death. Its literature is vivid and lyrical, yet many of the stories are parables of despair. These paradoxes make people uneasy.

The Civil War wrenched families apart and set brother against brother. It represented the ultimate psychic fault line between North and South and still creates aftershocks 150 years later. The war created another chasm, separating life in the South before 1861 from what came after. The abruptness and totality of this rift was unlike anything experienced in any other modern revolution. With a generation of men killed in battle or given their freedom; plantations, towns, and roads destroyed by General William T. Sherman's scorched-earth policy; and farms barren and unproductive, the white landowning class was suddenly, almost overnight, disenfranchised. In the words of Lyon Gardiner Tyler, son of President John Tyler of Sherwood Forest, Virginia, "Their past was severed from the present." In the summer of 1865, when author Augusta Jane Evans Wilson saw her publisher in Mobile, Alabama, he was distressed by her shabby appearance and suggested she buy some new attire. "Mr. Derby," the then-famous writer replied, "my father has lost everything; the slaves have been freed, and all our property confiscated. I have no money with which to replenish my wardrobe."

One of the far-reaching consequences of this dramatic change in fortunes, followed by the region's disastrous decline during Reconstruction and on into the beginning of the twentieth century, was the creation of what became an American myth—the myth of the Old South. Finding themselves in an economic and social wasteland after 1865, the families who had grown up in antebellum Dixie reinvented themselves as a society of aristocratic hedonists, living gracefully in a carefree, languorous climate, strolling through elegantly shaded plantation gardens full of live oaks hung with Spanish moss, redolent of the scent of magnolias. Today there are updated versions of the myth, and visitors to Pilgrimage Days in the South may drink mint juleps as they converse with Southern belles twirling parasols, dressed in crinolines and white gloves, or meet families who welcome tourists into houses filled with carefully displayed memorabilia—mini-theme parks of Gracious Southern Living.

But did these romantic visions of houses and gardens in the Old South ever actually exist? Or was all this just a post–Civil War dream to compensate for the painful reality of history?

Photographer Peter Woloszynski spent two years exploring the old plantation and family houses of the Southern states, stumbling on a wealth of unknown, unwritten biographies that transcended the clichés and revealed the authentic private world of the Old South, which he caught with his camera in an unprecedented visual record. As the writer, I followed in his footsteps two years later and rehearsed the stories of these families, almost all of whom were directly related to the original owners of the houses. Both the photographer and I are English, familiar with the tradition of great estates being passed down through generations. As foreigners, however, we were also free to come to an understanding of the history of these houses without political or emotional preconceptions. Our conclusions are drawn from our own, unbiased experience.

What we discovered was that there had indeed been a very specific way of life during this apogee of the South. Before the Civil War the great plantation families traveled to Europe, gave parties, collected art, and accumulated wealth. They built houses and filled them with treasures. All this took place over an extraordinarily short period of time, however. W. J. Cash writes in *The Mind of the South*, "It was 1800 before the advance of the plantation was really under way. . . . The whole period from the invention of the cotton gin to the outbreak of the Civil War is less than seventy years—the lifetime of a single man. Yet it was wholly within the longer of these periods, and mainly within the shorter, that the development and growth of the great South took place." (Virginia is an exception. Settled in the seventeenth century by a variety of disaffected English cavaliers and defeated Royalists, they brought to Virginia an elitist culture and produced a generation of educated and politically sophisticated "gentlemen" who ended up running the new American democracy.) Thus the myth of the Old South is based on fact but has actually been spun out of a history that lasted for less than half a century—a startlingly ephemeral golden age of approximately forty years.

But what a golden age it was! These people lived in a society of deep personal affinities—to one another, to their relations and neighbors (often the same), to their land, and, most of all, to their houses, which, like all personal palaces, reflected their builders' status and which, after the trauma of the Civil War, became their strongholds of identity, their dispensaries of memory.

The first and most striking attribute of these houses is their architecture. Built in that brief time frame of the early nineteenth century (almost all the houses portrayed in this book were built in the early 1800s), when most of the plantation owners became seriously rich and could express their wealth in conspicuous consumption, the mansions they built for themselves most often reflect a desire for authenticity and permanence. Although some went for the delightful ostentation of the Italianate style or the elegance of Georgian, many more chose Greek Revival architecture, thus making a direct reference to the classical orders and moral principles developed in the ancient world. Author Henry Wiencek probes deeper into the symbolism, believing that as tension between the North and the South increased, "the South drew comfort [in the face of Northern abolitionists] from its architectural association with an ancient and enduring civilization." Thus the fictional images of Tara and Twelve Oaks, the O'Hara and Wilkes plantations in *Gone with the Wind,* with their columns, pediments, pilasters, and porches, in fact portray an accurate picture of this short-lived Southern building boom.

As well as being constantly urged to uphold the high-minded values of the classical world, the architects of Southern plantation houses had also to contend with practical problems—in particular the climate. The South was then a land without air-conditioning. Many of the houses had to be raised off the ground to avoid the dampness inherent in the summertime humidity. Wraparound porches or verandas provided all-important shade in the open air. Inside, the arrangement of rooms, stairwells, and corridors was designed for maximum accessibility to the breezes.

The interior decoration of the houses carried equally strong associations. The furniture and furnishings followed the fashions that had swept America by the mid-nineteenth century—Empire chests and beds, Belter-style rosewood parlor sets with deeply tufted upholstery, English pier tables and silver services, French porcelain and landscape wallpapers, marble mantels and gilt valances imported from Italy. Added to these European flourishes were Afro-Caribbean pieces such as punkah fans (devices hung from a dining-room ceiling that when pulled back and forth provided a breeze and kept mosquitoes away from the food), and other exotic items, many originating in New Orleans and the islands.

Today nothing has changed. This combination of European and tropical decoration is found almost exclusively in the antebellum Southern interior.

However, we are exposed to something more in these rooms than the period-specific décor: a profusion of personal mementoes, from old dolls to faded invitations to a cotillion. They have little commercial value, yet the cabinets stuffed with old porcelain; the peeling leather-bound books; the piles of ornate, tarnished silver; the faded Confederate uniforms; the scrapbooks of sepia photographs, lace hearts, rusting crinoline hoops; the cobwebbed steamer trunks—these, far from being sad essays in nostalgia, are living, breathing proof of family history, possessions as identity. Strip the houses of these objects, and the inhabitants of these houses would be like amnesiacs, without a context.

According to statistics, many Americans move every five years from state to state, home to home, job to job, uprooting, buying or building a new house, starting afresh, eager each time, it seems, to eradicate the past. The subjects of this book, on the other hand, have stayed precisely where they, their parents, their grandparents, and often their great-great-grandparents were born.

For them to move is to die.

Their houses contain the connective tissue to their ancestors. Within the walls of these beloved old places, family history remains alive. For such people, to abandon their sanctuaries would be to destroy their sense of belonging. It would mean confronting the future alone, without a compass, bereft of community.

The individuals who live in the houses shown in this book know that danger only too well. That is why they are holding on to their brief moment of Southern glory the only way they know how, by protecting and keeping alive the places and objects where that glory resides. They speak of pieces of furniture, for instance, almost as though they were human, stroking the wood of a dining table, caressing the fabric of a chair, admiring an ancestor's portrait. We tell of a young woman in Walterboro, South Carolina, as she gazes fondly at a worn Empire chest in her dining room. "This is my great-grandfather's hunt chest," she explains. "I would miss so much without it. My entire life and all my memories are in this old scratched chest."

Every room, every piece of furniture, every door handle, every teacup has a story. Storytelling is an essential part of these people's lives, providing them with a rich and continuous source of drama. Just as Southern literature is infused with a kind of heat and intensity that sets it apart from that of the North, so these houses are repositories of exotic narratives that seem essentially Southern, retaining their vitality from constant retelling. As we listened to these stories during our journey through the South, we were reminded of Binx Bolling's aunt in Walker Percy's *The Moviegoer*: "All the stray pieces of the past, all that is feckless and gray about people, she pulls together into an unmistakable visage of the heroic or the craven, the noble or the ignoble. So strong is she that sometimes the person and the past are in fact transfigured by her. They become what she seems them to be." Yet it is this power of transfiguration that we ultimately came to question. While captivated by our hosts' tales, charmed by their friendliness, and overwhelmed by their commitment to the past, once outside their siren reach, we saw in the blood-red soil of the Deep South other lives that clamored to be recognized.

For when one writes about these antebellum houses and their stories, a shadow falls across the page. It is the shadow of slavery. It is not possible to describe the architecture of these places, the history of their construction or the provenance of their contents, without acknowledging the incalculable debt they owe to the slaves who provided the labor with which to finance them and who in many cases built them with their own hands. In an essay about Flannery O'Connor, Alice Walker describes the house in Milledgeville, Georgia, where the great Southern writer grew up. The town house, belonging to O'Connor's grandfather, was built by slaves, who made the bricks by hand. (The same is true of several houses in this book.) Walker reflects that these slaves were probably some of her own relatives, suffering amid the heat and mosquitoes to build the house. "Whenever I visit antebellum homes in the South," she writes, "with their spacious rooms, their grand staircases, their shaded back windows that, without the thickly planted trees, would look out onto the now vanished slave quarters in the back, this is invariably my thought. I stand in the backyard gazing up at the windows, then stand at the windows inside looking down into the backyard, and between the me that is on the ground and the me that is at the windows, History is caught."

Perhaps that is why the future of these houses is in doubt. Built on a shadow, they cannot last. They are monuments to an illusion, and all the stories ever told cannot in the end put back together the "stray pieces of the past." As in the poignant image of a parlor in Montgomery, Alabama, empty except for an old family portrait hanging in lonely splendor over the fireplace, the lifeblood of these places is gradually draining away.

Beautiful still, such houses are free at last, in the words of Southern writer Elizabeth Spencer, "to enter, with abandon, the land of mourning and shadows and memory." The families are hanging on as long as they can, almost impervious to the march of time. A favorite saying within this community of survivors is "Too poor to paint, too proud to whitewash." In some cases, the next generation, with renewed vigor and an infusion of cash, is moving in and taking on the enormous task of rescuing a beloved family home from destruction. Their houses are responding to this effort and taking on a new role for children and grandchildren. But it seems inevitable that for many of these houses, economic rigors, cultural pressures, and generational fatigue will ultimately bring the curtain down. After their disappearance, neither Tara nor Twelve Oaks will rise again. Meanwhile, in the photographs and stories collected in these pages, History, as Alice Walker says, is caught. We offer this book as a pictorial elegy to that vanished age.

VIRGINIA

I can shut my eyes now, after all these years, and
summon back the scene as vividly as I saw it when we emerged
from the long stretch of twilight. I can still see the blue glimmer
of the flowers in the grass; the low house, with deep wings,
where the stucco was peeling from the red brick beneath a delicate
tracery of Virginia creeper; the seven pyramidal cedars
guarding the hooded roof of gray shingles; and the clear afterglow
in which the little moon sailed like a ship.

—ELLEN GLASGOW, "WHISPERING LEAVES"

SHERWOOD FOREST
CHARLES CITY, VIRGINIA

*The front hall, in the old part of the house, opens into the dining room.
A portrait of Julia Gardiner Tyler hangs above a sofa that came from Payne
Tyler's home, Pine House Plantation, in South Carolina. It was in
this room that Julia Gardiner Tyler wrote most of her correspondence.*

The history of the great Southern plantations is also the history of the great rivers rolling down the Southern map of the United States. From the Mississippi in the west to the James River in the east, these important waterways fed the wealth of the plantation owners with their efficient trading posts and speed of communication from one side of the country to the other. Sherwood Forest is one of the beneficiaries of these alluvial currents. One of the four so-called James River Plantations, it is steeped in early American history, was home to the tenth president of United States, John Tyler, and has been in the same family for more than 150 years. What sets Sherwood Forest apart, however, is its extraordinary contemporary record of life in the house since before the Civil War, presented in the form of letters and documents belonging to the Tyler family, and now preserved in Virginia museums and libraries.

The Italian fruitwood pier table in the hall, dated 1844, was purchased by Julia Gardiner Tyler and taken to the White House. The anonymous portrait of President Tyler, painted during his term in office, is similar to one by G. P. A. Healy, which hangs in the White House.

The plantation has its origins in a 1616 land grant. Strategically situated thirty-five miles east of Richmond and eighteen miles west of Williamsburg, both important cities in colonial America, Walnut Grove, as it was then called, was a desirable location not only for its fertile soil but also for those interested in a political career. William Henry Harrison, ninth president of the United States, inherited a part of the property that would become Sherwood Forest in 1790, but its full flowering came with the purchase of the house in 1842 (along with sixteen hundred acres) by John Tyler, who, as vice president to Harrison, became the tenth—and first unelected—president when Harrison died after only thirty days in office. (Tyler had grown up only a few miles from Harrison's birthplace.)

Although conservative in his preference for living close to home, John Tyler was a controversial president, ever ready to vote against his party, the Whigs, when he found his own high principles at odds with the party line. In fact he renamed his house Sherwood Forest in recognition of his Robin Hood–like reputation as a political outlaw. Not the least of his unconventional acts was his marriage at the age of fifty-four in 1844, while still in office, to a twenty-four-year-old woman called Julia Gardiner (of the Gardiners Island Gardiners). His first wife died in 1842, after bestowing on him eight children, and the speed with which he married the second, let alone her age, raised more than a few eyebrows. If Tyler was regarded as a nonconformist, Julia Gardiner soon showed she was a match for her husband and that her youth was no impediment to her independence of spirit or self-confidence. On June 30, 1844,

OPPOSITE: *The architectural style of Sherwood Forest is known as Virginia Tidewater, owing to its location in the southeastern part of the state. It is the longest frame house in America, three hundred feet long.* ABOVE: *The library, the oldest room in the house, was used by President Tyler as his bedroom. On the far wall is a portrait of Payne Tyler's great-grandmother, surrounded by paintings from her family plantation, Mulberry Hill. The handmade rocking-horse is circa 1880.*

she wrote to her sister, Juliana, "I have commenced my auspicious reign and am in quiet possession of the Presidential
Mansion."

Quiet she may have been in Washington, but her brilliant
marriage to Tyler almost entirely shaped the ultimate history
of Sherwood Forest. It seems Tyler bought the house with the
idea of retiring there after his stormy presidency came to an
end in 1845. From 1842 on, he began making renovations, and
when Julia first saw the house on her honeymoon in 1844, she
wasted no time in bringing her own considerable talents to
the project. The house was originally a simple frame house,
dating from 1730 (the central three-story section still reflects its
age). It is only one room deep, like a very long railroad car.
Tyler, evidently energized by his new marriage, added one-
story wings to each side of the house, including a covered
walkway to connect the kitchen and laundry to the east end
and a west wing that became, like that in the White House,
his office. He put in a new staircase in the hall. He also
installed, no doubt at the instigation of his new and lively
dancing partner, a sixty-eight-foot-long ballroom (just the right
length for a Virginia reel), which Julia, when she first saw it,
decided would be greatly improved by a vaulted ceiling, to
make the music sound better. And so it did. Thus the house,
with the added ballroom and wings, was elongated to three
hundred feet, the longest frame house in America.

One of the most wonderful aspects of Sherwood Forest is
the extensive documentation preserved through the years cov-
ering John and Julia Tyler's life together. Julia and her family

wrote more than forty thousand letters to each other while she lived on the plantation, all of which survive, revealing a fascinating day-by-day description of her life. She was no shrinking violet when it came to claiming credit for the work on the house. "The head carpenter was amazed at my science and the president acknowledged I understood more about carpentry and architecture than he did and he would leave all arrangements that were to be made entirely to my taste." Julia had some reservations about renovating an old house as opposed to building a new one, but she declared firmly, "It will be the handsomest place in the County and I assure you there are some very fine ones in it."

Julia made sure that all the best furniture and furnishings were brought in from the United States and abroad. She was a keen shopper, and on her European travels before her marriage she purchased items such as the Italian landscape painting that now hangs in the drawing room. When in the White House, she had asked for an appropriation with which to buy furniture. The Congress offered her a paltry sum, so she went out and bought objects herself, and when President Tyler left office, she took her purchases with her. Some of them can still be seen in the rooms of Sherwood Forest.

It was not only the house she focused on. Julia was a highly educated, cultivated young woman and was as interested in gardens and landscape design as in the decorative arts. "The grove will be made into a park (twenty-five acres) and stocked with deer," she wrote to her sister in 1844. A year later: "The hyacinths, tulips, violets, cowslips and various

ABOVE: *The ghost room, where the Grey Lady tends to spend her time, was originally the nursery. A vintage petticoat that belonged to Payne Tyler's grandmother seems to accentuate the mysterious atmosphere.*
OPPOSITE: *In the second-floor hallway is a display of sporting objects, including Payne Tyler's riding boots and polo mallets.*

The deer, called George, was shot by Harrison Tyler. His wife painted the portrait above the desk, which is adjacent to the kitchen.

other flowers are blooming in our beds, and the peach trees are in full bloom." Julia's mother took a great interest in her daughters' horticultural efforts and promised to send her Andrew Jackson Downing's treatise on landscape design, the most popular book of the time on the subject. John Tyler shared his wife's interest, asking for two female statues to "preside over the garden" from the south piazza. Land clearing, planting lists, and pruning were frequently mentioned.

It is clear from their correspondence that John and Julia Tyler enjoyed a blissfully harmonious marriage, despite the age discrepancy. "She is all that I could wish her to be," he wrote, "the most beautiful woman of the age and at the same time the most accomplished." She was equally adoring. "It seemed as if I had stepped into paradise," she said of her honeymoon. Ten years later she observed, "The President is in good health, and cheerful, which is essential to good health. He fiddles away every evening for the little children black and white to dance to on the Piazza and seems to enjoy it as much as the children. I never saw a happier temperament than he possesses." Meanwhile, amid all the redecorating and Virginia reels, she produced for him seven children, bringing his total to fifteen.

However, as with all such elite families in the South, these happy times were not to last. "The prospects now are that we shall have a war, and a trying one," Tyler wrote to his wife on April 16, 1861. "These are dark times, dearest, and I think only of you and our little ones. . . . I shall vote secession." A year later, he died at the age of seventy-one. Soon there was a lot

of fighting along the James River, a critical supply route, and in 1864 Julia, now a young widow with seven children, decided to escape the continuing danger and take the family to New York. Shortly after she left, Sherwood Forest was raided. The Union soldiers were well aware of the wealth hoarded along the banks of the river. A surviving letter, poorly spelled and punctuated, records their bitter feelings. "This whole country is owned by heavy land holders owning from one to twenty thousand acres a poor man cant own any land." This same soldier reported entering President Tyler's house and "took and destroyed lots of stuff. They say he has the nicest kind of a mansion the house furnished in the best of style. They [took] some very nice furniture such as sofas, looking glasses, stands, carpeting, etc, of the very costliest kind and destroyed the pyana [sic] & large looking glasses & such other stuff . . ."

The house itself remained relatively unscathed. A burn mark on the floor of the hall is one of the few signs of the vandalism that took place.

Julia Tyler returned with her children to Sherwood Forest in 1867 and over the years continued to visit the plantation while also spending time in New York and Washington. She finally moved to Richmond in 1882, and died there in 1889. John and Julia Tyler's grandson, Harrison Ruffin Tyler, lives here today with his wife and family. This means that the direct genealogical link connecting President Tyler, born in 1790, to his grandson Harrison Tyler, born in 1928, extends nearly three hundred years.

Harrison Tyler and his wife, Payne, who came from another old Southern family, the Bettises, started restoring the house in the mid-1970s, after it had suffered a certain amount of neglect. Like Julia, her indomitable antecedent, Payne Tyler has made a great contribution to the interior of Sherwood Forest, not only by selecting appropriate wallpapers, furnishings, and paint but also by bringing in furniture from her own family plantations in South Carolina, Pine House and Mulberry Hill.

Many of the seventeenth- and eighteenth-century outbuildings remain, including a kitchen/laundry, smokehouse, milk house, and tobacco barn, as well as John Tyler's law office. Specimen trees still dominate the landscape, including a ginkgo tree given to John Tyler by Captain Matthew Perry in the late 1850s. Harrison, Payne, and their children continue to live in the house and take care of it. As is the case with many English stately homes, the family has designated part of the house to be open to the public while retaining the rest as their own private quarters.

In March 1845 Julia Tyler wrote proudly to her sister, "I have made a resolution never to go away from home except when I visit the North, or *certainly only where I have a particular preference.*" John Tyler shared her commitment to home and family. According to Robert Seager, author of *And Tyler Too,* the ex-president boasted that he was "not likely to let the [family] name become extinct." How gratified he would be if he were to visit Sherwood Forest in this new century and see the powerful connections between his own world and that inhabited today by his remarkable descendants.

Payne Tyler's family bed is kept in a bedroom on the third floor along with children's clothes that have been kept in a trunk since 1896

BLACK WALNUT FARM

RANDOLPH, VIRGINIA

Much of the furniture in the parlor was passed down from the Simms family. The Chickering piano came with the house. The prints of Lee (dated 1870) and Jackson (dated 1872) are rare.

The Piedmont area of Virginia,
near the North Carolina border, is traditionally
known as Southside Virginia and was once dominated
by the tobacco-growing counties of Halifax and
Mecklenberg. Black Walnut Farm was built in the
1770s by the Simms family, who bought thirty-three
hundred acres in Halifax County for eight shillings.
The Simmses and their heirs lived on a farm for over
two hundred years, during the most difficult times in
Southern history, before finally handing it over to
their relatives, the Watkins family, in 1985.
Before the Civil War the farm worked tobacco, wheat,
corn, hogs, and oxen and became quite prosperous,
with a large slave population. Then came the war.
The Simms family chose to stay away from the
fighting, and Black Walnut Farm escaped damage,
thanks in part to a remarkably brave stand by
Confederate soldiers only a few minutes' ride from

In the library there are shelves of books on surgery, an ancestor's
preoccupation, along with family photographs.

The Empire chest of drawers comes from the Watkins family, as does the mirror and the silver collection beneath it. On the table are family pieces from Tucker's mother, who came from New Orleans.

the house. The confrontation took place at the Staunton River Bridge battlefield, where, on a sizzling hot day in June 1864, 492 old men and young boys (all who were left by this time), held the bridge against three thousand Union cavalry and artillery.

The Simmses hung on to Black Walnut Farm, doing as best they could under severely reduced circumstances. However, when their descendants finally decided to sell in 1985, they sold it to relatives. "My father bought the farm fifteen years ago," says Tucker Watkins, who lives here now, "and that was the first time it had changed hands since the original purchase."

Tucker Watkins's own ancestors ran a ferry at Watkins Bridge and prospered, settling in Charlotte County, a little to

the north. They built three fine houses, named Do-Well, Do-Better, and Do-Best. (Only Do-Well survives.) Tucker's maternal great-grandfather, William Barksdale, then only sixteen years old, was one of those fighting to hold the Staunton River bridge. Tucker's paternal great-grandfather also participated in the war. Tucker recently found a letter in a desk in Black Walnut Farm written by his namesake, young Tucker Watkins, to his father on July 13, 1863, from an encampment in North Carolina. "This has been one of the darkest hours of the Confederacy," the boy writes. "Vicksburg has been taken by the Yankees. The garrison was starved was the reason why they had to surrender." He adds toward the end, "I think I will have to put off marrying until the war is over."

The dining room is one of the later additions, built around 1800. The decorative wallpaper dates from the 1920s. The portrait over the fireplace is of Judge Barksdale. The valances are gilded wood.

Black Walnut Farm is not a plantation mansion, but a modest house, with probably three additions dating up to the 1850s, as the family expanded. The kitchen and sitting room, with pine wainscoting and low doorways, are from the earliest period of the house, as can be confirmed by the kitchen windows, which date from the 1700s. By the 1800s larger rooms were added, with higher ceilings. "By that time, they could afford to heat them better," Tucker explains. Prior to the outbreak of the Civil War, the Simms family had done well enough to make more extensions. The house now has twelve fireplaces. A second staircase was also added, creating twin hallways.

Since the Watkinses moved in, the interior of Black Walnut Farm has become a repository of Watkins family heirlooms. The rooms retain many memories of both of Tucker's great-grandfathers, particularly William Barksdale, who became a judge at the age of twenty-five and had a long and distinguished career in the county. In the house is the bed in which he was born. Most of the furniture and furnishings come from

ABOVE: *A print of Robert E. Lee is flanked by a set of glass candelabras and other family mementoes.* ABOVE LEFT: *Family photographs are guarded by an eagle holding up a glass-globed lamp.* OPPOSITE: *The collection of dolls belonged to Tucker Watkins's grandmother Louise Watkins Barksdale.*

LEFT: *Amongst the group of outbuildings are a cool house (on the left) and a working smokehouse (on the right). Bullet, the family dog, stands guard.* BELOW: *Defined by a picket fence, a small henhouse, with a steep roof that matches those of the other outbuildings, nestles in front of old slave quarters.*

the Watkins family, including Tucker's mother, who came from New Orleans.

Tucker tells the story of wanting to hang prints of Robert E. Lee and Stonewall Jackson in the house. However, the families of many ex-slaves still live on the property. "This was their place too," he observes. So he asked them if they minded about the pictures. "This house is history," they told him. "These prints are history." The prints stayed.

The history of Black Walnut Farm is not complete without reference to another, more mysterious presence in this house. "We call it the Haunted Room," Tucker says of one of the large upstairs bedrooms. "There have been three incidents that cannot be explained. Pieces of furniture falling, bedclothes moving, sheets strangely tucked in." His niece, who frequently comes to visit, now refuses to sleep in that room.

Tucker Watkins farms six hundred acres today, with hay, wheat, tobacco, and a few pigs. One of Black Walnut Farm's most interesting aspects is the series of small outbuildings in the backyard of the house that once provided the infrastructure of a large working farm. All these structures have been meticulously restored. Tucker has installed a picket fence to frame these little houses and barns. To the north side of the house is another ghost of sorts: A large area of boxwood lines a series of small pathways, clearly forming the pattern of what was once a formal terraced parterre, with specimen trees and shrubs that date back to the 1800s. Near this shadowed tracery of a garden, along with the cedars of Lebanon, spruces and hollies are the old black walnuts that gave the farm its name.

In the dining room, a white glass-fronted cabinet holds heirloom glass and china.

THE WOODLANDS
BRODNAX, VIRGINIA

*The Federal mirror at the far end of the parlor, dating from
the 1800s, is older than the room. The curtains are original. The chandelier
was made to match the one in the library, as was the mantel.
The parlor set is typical Rococo Revival.*

The Woodlands, with its handsome Greek Revival façade, twenty-four-foot-high fluted columns, and post-and-rail fencing, overlooking a lush Virginian landscape dotted with horses swishing their tales in the sunshine, seems the archetypal plantation house from history and fiction. However, like so many antebellum houses in the South, the Woodlands developed from modest origins, and only after at least a hundred years did it become the fine mansion standing today. § The Woodlands was built around 1746 as an overseer's house. Various architectural clues in the original dining room—the old window moldings, the low front door, the carving of the mantel, the little staircase off the main room—indicate the layout of a much smaller house than the present one. § The first recorded owner was a Benjamin Harrison, about whom little is known except that with him the property was expanded to several thousand acres. William Edward Brodnax bought the house from the Harrison family between 1799 and 1807. He also began to buy up land in the area, until it added up to more

One of the finest examples of Greek Revival architecture in the South, The Woodlands stands on a small incline overlooking the lush Virginia countryside.

than four thousand acres. That he was an important and prosperous citizen is indicated by the fact that Brodnax is also the name of the town where the house is situated, at the southernmost border of the state. William Brodnax died in 1831, and the house was inherited by his daughter, Ann Brodnax Wilkins. The first stage of building began then, as her husband, John Wilkins, made improvements on the house for his family. Mrs. Wilkins died prematurely in 1833, and John brought his widowed sister and three children to live with him.

As family members either died or dispersed, by the early 1850s the house had been vacant for several years, until Dr. Alexander John Brodnax, a nephew of John Wilkins, moved in. In 1854, Dr. Brodnax married a young woman from Philadelphia, Ellen Mallory, and they immediately began an extensive remodeling program of the house. Mrs. Brodnax clearly had strong ideas about what a plantation house should look like (it has been suggested that the well-known architect Samuel Sloan was a consultant), and under her watch the grand Greek Revival portico was added, thus creating a new front entrance and interior hallway along with a new parlor or drawing room At the back of the house a small doctor's office was built, where Dr. Brodnax might see patients.

Dr. Brodnax inherited the house outright in 1861, not an auspicious year in the memory of the South. He immediately went off to fight for the Confederacy, leaving his formidable Northern-born wife to fight her own small war against the Union army, which had set up camp in White Plains, a town about three miles from the Woodlands. The story has it that

The hall, which was added to the original house in the mid-eighteenth century, is well situated to receive cool drafts, as well as having thick insulating walls on each side. The mirror and grandfather clock come from the Randolph family.

ABOVE: *In the living room, dating from 1746, most of the furniture is original. The portrait is of Sally Brodnax.* RIGHT: *The library is one of the original rooms of the house. It has an original chandelier and a marble mantel.*

RIGHT: A family photograph of a cleric sits near a dinner bell. BELOW: When the parlor was added in the 1850s, the Rococo-style parlor set was bought new for the room. The handsome mirror is of the same date. OPPOSITE: The mantel in the living room is original, and the mirror, though restored, has "always been here." OPPOSITE BELOW LEFT: The walnut dining table, circa 1812, comes from Bolling Randolph's mother. The sideboard was called a "sugar table" by Bolling's grandmother. OPPOSITE BELOW RIGHT: Leather-bound books of eclectic subject matter.

ABOVE: *A window in the barn reflects the back of the house in one of the old glass panes.*
OPPOSITE: *Old outbuildings serve as storage and workspace for this busy horse-breeding farm.*

Ellen Mallory Brodnax made contact with the commanding officer, General Hugh Boyle Ewing, in order to protect her home and possessions, only to discover that she and the general had been acquaintances in Philadelphia. Thanks to this connection, the Union soldiers left the Woodlands alone.

The Brodnaxes had two children, but only one, Nelly, survived, and she inherited the house in 1913 after her mother died. (Dr. Brodnax died in 1885.) Nelly was a Roman Catholic and added a Catholic chapel to the grounds of the house. She never married, and bequeathed the house to her cousin Henry Stuart Lewis. After Mrs. Lewis died, the plantation came into the hands of her daughter, Sue Bolling Randolph Meredith, and then to her son, Bolling Randolph, who lives there now with his wife, Kay, and their five children. "I grew up here," Bolling says, "and we moved in when my mother died in 1994."

Nothing much has changed inside the house since Dr. and Mrs. Brodnax made their prewar additions. Furniture from Bolling's relatives fill the rooms, mostly dating from the early to mid-1800s. He cannot remember some of their origins, but they are definitely Virginian. "My family tree is so interconnected, it goes back to practically everyone in the state," he says.

The farm now consists of 310 acres, producing tobacco and cotton. The Randolphs' major activity, however, is horse breeding, and they send their hunter-jumpers all over the country. The Randolphs also recently bought the village store, which they run themselves. "It's a busy life," Bolling says, adding a sentiment echoed by so many of these great old plantation owners. "It's hard these days to stay on the farm."

THE
CAROLINAS

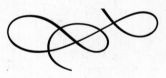

*The Southern gentleman is not
circumscribed in the construction of his house, or the
laying out of gardens and lawns.*

—SAMUEL SLOAN, CIRCA 1852

COOLEEMEE PLANTATION

ADVANCE,
NORTH CAROLINA

*The dramatic spiral staircase of the house winds up to the top of the
tower; the central cupola sucks up hot air and leaves cooler temperatures below.*

At its height before the Civil War, the Cooleemee (pronounced COO-luh-mee) Plantation in North Carolina's Piedmont region consisted of forty-two hundred acres of tobacco-producing land. This was but one of forty-five plantations owned at that time by the Hairston family in North and South Carolina, Virginia, and Mississippi. Like many Southern families, the Hairstons were Scottish by descent and careful, in true Scottish fashion, with money—hence their vast landholdings and equally vast fortunes. As in so many Southern stories, however, destiny was to deal a harsh hand to this family and this beautiful place. The present owner, North Carolina state judge Peter Wilson Hairston, now in his eighties, with the support of his wife, Lucy, has managed through dedication and hard work to retrieve from disaster a house that over the years has witnessed a long saga of economic reversal and human frailty.

A view of the house showing the unusual plan of wings—there are four—radiating out from the central core, topped by an octagonal tower.

The judge's great-great-great-grandfather Peter Hairston bought the land here for twenty thousand dollars in 1817. On his death in 1832, he left it to his grandson Peter, who was only thirteen years old. The Hairstons were deeply committed to the soil, and young Peter, while getting a proper education and grand tour in Europe, always knew that the tobacco fields of the plantation would ultimately summon him home.

As was the custom in many Southern families, he married his cousin, Columbia Stuart, and in 1852 started building a new house on Cooleemee land for his growing family. The architect he selected was William H. Ranlett from New York, whose work was featured in a journal he published called *The Architect*. According to family legend, Columbia's brother, the dashing Jeb Stuart, later to gain fame for his courage in the Civil War, was interested in architecture and wanted to find a suitable plan for the Hairstons, but had found nothing but a "Gothic coop." In the meantime, one of Ranlett's designs was reprinted in the January issue of *Godey's Lady's Book* of 1850, and this was what the Hairstons chose.

The design consisted of four wings radiating out from an octagonal core, in the center of which a dramatic spiral staircase uncoiled upward to a glass-topped cupola. Although unusual, the architect's plan was thoroughly practical; the cross-drafts from the opposing windows of the four wings provided cooling breezes in the summer, while the height of the hall allowed the space to act like a flue, sucking the hot air up to the top of the staircase, leaving cooler air to circulate below. Three hundred thousand bricks were made on the site

ABOVE: *A fine mirror and pier table, flanked by family portraits and a pair of elaborately carved Victorian chairs, dominate the large entrance hall.* OPPOSITE: *The portrait of Sammy Hairston, Judge Hairston's father's half-brother, as a young boy, was painted in 1854 by William G. Browne. He surveys the scene at the base of the finely carved hall staircase.*

RIGHT: *The sheet music on the piano was bought around 1900 by "Miss Fanny," the Judge's formidable grandmother.* OPPOSITE: *Family photographs crowd every surface. "The past is part of our present," says Judge Hairston.*

PREVIOUS PAGE LEFT: *The parlor is sparsely furnished, showing off two rare rugs brought back from Turkey by one of the Judge's forebears. Two French gilt mirrors, bought in 1856 when the house was first furnished, face off against each other on opposite walls.* PREVIOUS PAGE TOP RIGHT: *In a bay window off the living room, Ionic columns guard a modern chest. The Persian prayer rug was brought back from Turkey by Judge Hairston's father-in-law.* PREVIOUS PAGE BOTTOM RIGHT: *The dining room is dominated by a large mahogany-framed mirror. Some Hairston silver, dating back 150 years, sits on the sideboard.*

for the house's exterior and interior. Ionic columns, marble and walnut detailing, family portraits, and rich fabrics enhanced the luxurious ornamentation of the house.

Shortly after this splendid structure had been completed, Columbia died in childbirth, and later her three other children also died. Peter remarried and had more children, but history and politics were to jeopardize their prosperity. In April 1861, while at Cooleemee, Peter heard that Virginia had seceded from the Union. He made a terse entry in his diary: "Went to war. Kept no further accounts."

At the end of the Civil War, Cooleemee met the fate of many similar plantations. With the hundreds of Hairston slaves (many also called Hairston) set free, the place could no longer function. The unhappy period known as Reconstruction forced Peter, afraid of the dangerous atmosphere, to move with his wife and four children to Baltimore. He never returned to Cooleemee.

Peter Hairston died after having lost almost all the family fortune in honoring a partner's bad debt. In reduced circumstances, Peter's widow and children decided to return home to the South. They were determined to bring Cooleemee back to

life. It was a long and fruitless struggle. When Judge Peter Hairston finally inherited the house from his mother in 1963, the house was in derelict condition. He and his wife, Lucy, gave up their careers to share the burden and joy of restoring their beloved Cooleemee as best they could, as well as trying to make the land once more profitable.

The task was huge. The roof needed replacing, the plasterwork was crumbling, the garden had almost disappeared. But there was no question in the judge's mind, even though the once-prosperous Hairstons had been brought to their knees, that the plantation must survive. They fixed the roof and restored the plaster, and Lucy set to work on bringing back the garden, including a hundred-year-old boxwood walk. While involved in this project, Hairston was appointed to the Superior Court of North Carolina, the result of twenty-five years of law practice and three terms in the state legislature.

Their commitment paid off. Under Lucy's guidance, the garden was reclaimed. Electricity had been belatedly introduced in 1939 to replace the more romantic candlelight (when the judge's father complained he could no longer see what he was eating), and tobacco was replaced by corn, soybeans, cotton, and stands of pine trees. In 1978 the U.S. Department of the Interior declared Cooleemee a National Historic Landmark. Peter's son and two grandchildren, the seventh and eighth generations of Hairstons at Cooleemee, have been assuming the burden and continuing the enormous work a house like this will always need.

Perhaps even more significant than the revival of the prop-

erty is the revitalization of the Hairston name. In a prize-winning study of the family entitled *The Hairstons: An American Family in Black and White*, author Henry Wiencek traces the history of the African American Hairston families as they worked their way out of the past and claimed their heritage. The judge now meets his black namesakes (and in some cases relatives) regularly at reunions. Perhaps that is why the atmosphere of this house is so evocative. The family treasures speak not only of lost fortunes but also of endurance, understanding, and hope, and Cooleemee's painful history has, it seems, been finally reconciled in a handshake.

A cabinet holds china, glasses, dishes, and pitchers that have been collected by the Hairstons for many years.

McLEOD HOUSE
WALTERBORO, SOUTH CAROLINA

The first-floor veranda has a balustrade and doors with transoms and shutters. The doors, which are no longer used, each contain four large windowpanes made of the original glass.

Walterboro is called the jewel
of the low country of South Carolina. Inland from
Charleston and Savannah, the house was built in the
late eighteenth century by families looking for a
summer retreat from the intense heat and mosquito-
infested climate of the southeastern seaboard, where
the big plantation houses mostly stood. The first
families here grew rice, but Colleton County is
covered in rich forests, and many plantation owners
turned to timber instead. There are no rice fields left
today. Timber remains the largest business in the
region. Meanwhile, the three-hundred-year-old oaks,
pines, cedars, and cypress that dominate the domestic
landscape offer invaluable shade in the summertime.

*The McLeod house displays its beautiful Southern provenance, with verandas on
the first and second floors wrapped with delicate wood balustrades.
The early-nineteenth-century Greek Revival–influenced
façade is surrounded by azaleas, pine trees, magnolias, and live oaks.*

ABOVE AND OPPOSITE: *The living room has unusual tongue-and-groove walls and ceiling. The furniture is mostly rosewood with tufted upholstery. The windows are draped in elegant damask curtains. The chandelier was made for the room, and the carved wood fireplace with black marble trim is original to the house. Above the mantel is a portrait of Rhoda Lane McLeod, Gordon McLeod's mother.*

Walterboro has many charming antebellum houses, but the McLeod house stands out not only for its position as the highest house in town—seventy-five feet above sea level—but also as the oldest house that is still inhabited. Built in 1820 or earlier, it sits proudly on a six-acre rise, the long driveway shaded by huge oaks draped in Spanish moss, pines, and magnolias and lined with massive azalea bushes. Such houses were called high houses, because they were built high enough to escape the worst of the mosquitoes. Moreover, without air-conditioning, the high ground offered the opportunity to catch a breeze. The extensive planting of the large shade trees also served far more than an aesthetic purpose.

The mahogany Regency chest in the dining room came from the McLeod family. The blue and white Chinese tureen belonged to Colonel Isaac Hayne, a revolutionary war hero from South Carolina who is buried at Hayne Hall, the family seat near Walterboro. Above it is a portrait of Gordon McLeod's grandmother, aged twelve.

In all its long life, the house has had only three owners: the Glovers, an old Walterboro family who built it; the Warleys; and then the McLeods, who acquired it in 1937. Gordon McLeod was born in the house. His mother was a schoolteacher and his father was a prominent lawyer. When Gordon's mother died, he and his wife, Terry, moved into the house. Terry is also from an old Walterboro family, the Boyntons—even older, she points out, than the McLeods. "We had a rice plantation here." Like many Southern women, she sacrificed her own world to that of her husband's and now deals with the McLeod family history as though it were her own. "That's the right thing to do," she declares. "We know about inheritance. We know about the houses coming to us and prepare accordingly."

The architecture of the McLeod house illustrates the simple style of its early date, with Greek Revival elements such as the columns and balustrades. There is a handsome second-story verandah and a low-pitched roof made of tin. ("I love it when it rains. I tell my husband to turn the TV off at night so I can listen to it thunder down on the roof," Terry McLeod says.)

The windows facing onto the porch, framed by black shutters, are unusually long, with original glass panes. Two French doors (which no longer open) flank the front door. All three have matching glass transoms. Like many Southern houses, this one looks solid to the core, but when a building is this old, impressions are not worth much. The McLeods recently discovered to their horror that the twelve-foot-thick heart pine beams under the porch supporting the house had shrunk, because of termites, to less than a foot.

The interior of the McLeod house is as elegant and unpretentious as its exterior. The most significant decorative feature is the woodwork, made locally, which is of the highest quality. The walls and ceilings in the living and dining rooms are tongue-and-groove. Beautifully carved beading radiates out from the center of the ceilings, creating the effect almost of a tent. The chandeliers in both rooms were made for the house. Most of the rooms contain furniture belonging to the McLeods, some of the pieces dating back to the Civil War, when they were packed away and luckily survived.

Furniture is of vital importance to this family. When

The dining room also has tongue-and-groove walls and ceiling, with the addition of a simple molding on the ceiling that forms a diamond. The dining table came from the Boynton family. The portrait is of Walter James McLeod, Jr., a naval officer.

Gordon McLeod's mother died, her furniture was to be divided up between her children, but four years later the parceling out has still to be completed. It seems that some family decisions are too difficult to make without much time and reflection. Terry, who waits to see how the final dispositions will be made, has meanwhile brought some furniture from her family to join her husband's collection, and these additions are very important to her. She points with particular affection to a large Empire chest in the dining room. "This is my great-grandfather's hunt chest, where he kept his guns, knives, and ammunition," she explains. "It's scratched and nicked but I love it." She also singles out an armoire in the bedroom. "It has a crack in it," she says, caressing it, "but to me it's beautiful." Terry is articulating a particularly Southern perception that many people fail to recognize—that old things can convey meanings that touch the heart. For Terry, her family furniture is part of her identity, and without it she does not feel complete. "I would miss so much without it," she says. "My entire life and all my memories are in this old scratched chest."

From the veranda, the view of the estate stretches out through the ancient woods. To the right of the house is a small, walled formal garden.

MISSISSIPPI

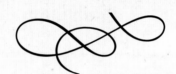

The galleries ran the full width of the house back and front, and under the roof's low swing, the six slender posts along the front stood hewn four-square and even-spaced by rule of a true eye. Pegs in the wood showed square as thumbnails along the seams; in the posts, the heart-grain rose to the touch. The makings of the house had never been hidden to the Mississippi air, which was now, this first Sunday in August, and at this hour, still soft as milk.

—EUDORA WELTY, "LOSING BATTLES"

PALOMA PLANTATION & HAYNE HALL
GREENWOOD, MISSISSIPPI

Much of the furniture in the Hayne Hall parlor came from New Orleans. The central round table is rosewood with a marble top; it came from the Barnwell side of the family. The walls are the original plaster.

The town of Greenwood lies at the heart of the great Mississippi Delta, where many of the fabulous cotton empires were founded. Eighty-two miles north of the state capital, Jackson, the Yalobusha and Tallahatchie Rivers meet at Greenwood and form the Yazoo River, which snakes through the Delta flatlands in a parallel course with the Mississippi, following the line of hills from Memphis to Vicksburg through the great alluvial valley until it flows into its big sister at the Louisiana border. Although not a major player in the Civil War, Greenwood holds one of the only two Confederate memorial museums in the United States.

In the butter-colored dining room in Hayne Hall, the table and chairs are English Regency, dating from 1820. The Steinway piano is rosewood and came from North Carolina around 1850. The ceiling beams and moldings came from an old house in the area and were added by Simpson Hemphill.

LEFT: *Crimson clover serves a new function in a Victorian jar of what once contained "bosom pads."* OPPOSITE: *The ornately carved fretwork baluster in Hayne Hall is enhanced by a set of Indian prints that lines the stair's ascent.* BELOW: *The chairs on the upper landing are copies of Spanish Colonial ceba wood chairs bought in Guatemala.*

TOP: *Antique maps hang above a marble-topped table with an assortment of family mementoes.* ABOVE: *A case of rum bottles hand-blown in the late 1700s came originally from the West Indies.*

The original Paloma Plantation belonged to the great-grandparents of Simpson Hemphill, who lives here now. When his great-grandmother Harriet Butler Hayne married Edward Hazzard Barnwell, life was not easy. "It was a jungle here in 1850," Simpson points out. "You lived in the Delta and died of yellow fever. This house was built in the middle of a cotton field, where the river lost the battle with the land." When Simpson's grandfather ran the plantation, there were forty-five hundred acres of land. Now it is down to fifteen hundred acres, and it focuses on livestock and timber.

In 1929, the date Simpson Hemphill was born, the house was rebuilt for Simpson's parents. "Six generations of the family have sat in this living room," he remarks, looking 'round at the mementoes that surround him. "I love heritage and history and how people arrived in places," he admits. "My five times great-grandfather, Isaac Hayne, was hanged in 1781 by the British for siding with the Americans during the Revolutionary War. The first Barnwells came here in 1701, originally from Alabama." James Hemphill, Simpson's paternal ancestor, came from Ireland, fought in the revolution, and moved to Mississippi. It was a profitable move. "The Indians ceded land to the U.S. government in the 1830s," Simpson Hemphill explains, "just in time for my ancestors to reap the harvest of King Cotton."

Simpson's maternal grandfather, Edward Barnwell, also benefited from the cotton boom and became very prosperous. After the Civil War, like many other Southerners, he became aware of the vital role the women of the Confederate army had played, by staying behind and keeping the plantations

The back sitting room at Hayne Hall was formerly a rear porch.
The fireplace is pine; the door frame is walnut. A collection of early Northern
European maps decorates the walls.

ABOVE: *The back hall is illuminated by a stained-glass panel rescued from an old school (the colors represent the seasons). In the rustic glass cabinet are books, baskets, and family keepsakes.* OPPOSITE: *Paloma is packed with collections of Sheffield silver and Natchez china, plus old glass, wedding presents, and other mementoes inherited by Simpson from his grandmother.*

running. In the aftermath, with so many husbands and sons dead and gone, Mr. Barnwell created a foundation for such women, to help support them during the difficult days of Reconstruction. The Barnwell Fund, now well over one hundred years old, is still in operation.

In 1972, Simpson Hemphill bought a beautiful Greek Revival house a few miles from Paloma Plantation. The lower floor of the house was built in 1843, and the upper story was added in the 1850s. Simpson named the house Hayne Hall, in honor of his great-great-grandfather, who is buried, along with Simpson's father and grandfather, in the local cemetery.

The architecture of the house is a story in itself. The eight exterior columns are a lofty twenty-two feet high, hand-planed and tapered one inch from bottom to top, providing the same dramatic trick of perspective as the Parthenon columns constructed in Athens by the ancient Greeks. The federal-style pilasters each side of the front door came from a Barnwell family house in Beaufort, South Carolina. "We made them fit," Simpson says. The wooden fretwork balustrades around the front porch and second-floor balusters are original, carved in the 1850s. (The interior stair banisters are of the same date.) The color of the façade, a delicate yellow with white trim, was copied from a house in Charleston that Simpson saw and liked. He painted the tin roof red and the shutters dark green.

In decrepit condition when Simpson acquired it (the second story was not even wired for electricity), the interior of Hayne Hall, like the exterior, was slowly bought back to life by its new owner. Simpson added interior beams and door

ABOVE: *A favorite needlepoint pillow.* OPPOSITE TOP LEFT: *The West bedroom has a mahogany New Orleans bed and an Empire dressing table. The mantel is original.* OPPOSITE TOP RIGHT AND BOTTOM: *In the East bedroom, a silver brush set is assembled on an Empire chest. A set of camellia prints hangs on the wall. Originally the walls were plastered; now they are stained wood. The bed is walnut, bought in New Orleans and shipped to the house along with the parlor furniture.*

moldings that came from an old house in the area. Filled with English and American furniture, paintings, china, and silver, the house is now a hymn to the fine craftsmanship that was at its height in the early nineteenth century. Pieces from New Orleans, Indiana, and as far as Guatemala, Natchez china, needlepoint screens stitched by Simpson's grandmother, and stained glass Simpson rescued from an old local school all combine to give these rooms their idiosyncratic beauty. Almost everything comes from Simpson's family, including linens monogrammed with his grandmother's initials; hundred-year-old wedding presents; and an antique English picnic basket containing its original enamelware, tin tea canisters, and kerosene burner. In the west bedroom, the wardrobe still stands where Simpson's grandmother kept a bottle of sherry

for a private nip every now and then. ("A common practice," Simpson chuckles, "for women who were not expected to take a drink in public.")

People call this marvelous house Simpson's Playhouse, but Hayne Hall is something more—his life's work, the ultimate expression of his Southern family history. "We are not a transient people," he observes. "I still sleep in the same room where I was born." Between Hayne Hall and Paloma, where he lives most of the time, he keeps very busy. "I was spoiled as a boy," he says, "and my mother lived till she was ninety-nine years old. There was always someone picking up after me. But now I have to keep up the houses and the farm." He smiles at the thought. "I have fifty goats to look after," he adds. "And I've got 'em all named."

ABOVE: *The original Paloma house dates from the 1850s, and was rebuilt in 1929 for Simpson Hemphill's parents when he was born.* OPPOSITE: *The lovely façade of Hayne Hall, its yellow a color copied from a house in Charleston, the shutters dark green, and the columns twenty-two feet high, topped by a Greek Revival pediment. The upstairs balcony was added in the 1850s.*

CEDAR HILL
CARROLLTON, MISSISSIPPI

An old barn on the grounds of Cedar Hill contains family riding habits dating back many years—including those for a sidesaddle.

Carrollton is a tiny community nestled in the hills a few miles east of Greenwood. Its green, rolling topography stands in sharp contrast to the vast, flat expanse of rich Delta bottomland that ends at the foot of these hills. Like the other small towns of Carroll County (named in honor of Charles Carroll of Carrollton, Maryland, one of the signers of the Declaration of Independence), it was built on a foundation of cotton. For a time these communities flourished. Middleton, eight miles from Carrollton, became such a center of culture that it was known as the Athens of Mississippi. Its fame, however, was short-lived. Like many of the others, it had completely disappeared by the end of the nineteenth century. A cemetery is the only memorial left to Middleton's once thriving community.

A view of the entrance hall shows a long English country bench, and a painting of Mount Vernon above it. The wide heart pine floors were made for the house. Fine original moldings frame the doors.

ABOVE: *Books on antiques and Southern history, along with family photographs, are crowded in a bedroom.* OPPOSITE: *The dining room has wallpaper copied from the original, a mahogany dining table, an Empire mirror, and a set of Caribbean plantation chairs. The silver comes from the family.*

After the Civil War the Mississippi Central Railroad was directed through a new town, Winona, not far from Carrollton. Unlike Middleton, however, Carrollton, as the county seat of Carroll County, remained a popular place to live. It was better located than some of the lower-lying river towns, and people often summered here in order to take advantage of the cool air and escape the very real threat posed by the frequent outbreaks of malaria and yellow fever so common in the Mississippi Delta. Today its citizens still enjoy its refreshing breezes and lush vegetation.

Cedar Hill is owned by descendants of one of the first families of Carroll County, the Gee family. The first Gees arrived in Virginia from England in 1704. In 1841, like so many other Virginians, the family was lured to Mississippi by the promise of fertile land and the high price of cotton. Peter (1803–1883) and Mary Anne Moore Gee settled first in Middleton. Their son, Joseph James Gee, was born in 1834 and educated there. He then entered into a business partnership with Robert Leroy Bingham.

After the war the Gee family moved to Carrollton, the county's capital. In 1868 Joseph James Gee married Charlie Augusta Kimbrough, and they had six children. One son, Orman Kimbrough Gee, was the grandfather of the present generation, Anne Gee McGee and her brother, Joseph J. Gee III, who own and operate J. J. Gee & Sons, the family's dry goods store. The store, founded in 1880, is reputed to be the oldest general merchandise store continuously operated by the same family in the state of Mississippi.

A wig-stand displays a collection of silver-backed brushes accumulated by the Gee family.

The hill on which Cedar Hill sits was originally owned by the Bingham family, who were related to the Gees through business and marriage. The Binghams built a large house on this lovely site in the nineteenth century, but it burned down in the early twentieth century. In 1939 Joseph J. Gee II and his wife, Anne Strudwick Gee, purchased Cedar Hill and raised their two children here. The original structure was a "dog-trot" house, that is, a two-room house with a porch on both sides and a central connecting passageway. This layout, developed in response to the hot, humid southeastern climate, provided very efficient ventilation. The house was moved to its present location and attached to an existing structure. These two separate buildings were then incorporated under one roof.

Cedar Hill remains a simple one-story house, painted white

with dark green shutters. The original front porch and portico are in the Greek Revival style and feature fine examples of octagonal columns. The roof, with its unusual cupola, reflects a Mediterranean influence. A new wing and screened porch were added in the early 1950s. Thanks to the late Anne Strudwick Gee's keen eye for historical and architectural detail, the new wing melds imperceptibly with the old.

The interior is simple, as befits a cottage. Though small, the rooms are well proportioned. The entrance hall was obtained by enclosing a breezeway that once connected the two rooms of the original dog-trot structure. The flooring is made of wide heart pine boards original to the house, and the doors and windows are surrounded by elegant moldings. Furniture and furnishings consist of items passed down over several generations of both sides of the family (including por-

In a glass-topped table cabinet there is a selection of silver, mother-of pearl, and Boulle pieces, plus family objects and mementoes.

CLOCKWISE FROM RIGHT: *This view of the living room, shows the fine English mahogany corner cupboard and walls covered in grass cloth made in China. In the kitchen is a "biscuit break"—a nineteenth-century appliance with which one kneads dough through a crank and then rolls it out on the marble surface. The silhouettes are of famous American politicians John C. Calhoun and Martin Van Buren. Icons from Greece decorate the living room walls. Casually gathered gauze curtains keep breezes flowing in the bedroom. Family portraits decorate the walls.*

traits and silver collections), as well as items collected by Anne Strudwick Gee, who was a knowledgeable antiques collector and dealer.

Cedar Hill does not possess the grandeur or pretensions of the large antebellum plantation houses still admired throughout much of the Old South. However, the history of Cedar Hill is inextricably linked to the history of the state of Mississippi. Through the stewardship of the present generation, Anne McGee and Joseph J. Gee III are preserving the past while ensuring that Cedar Hill remains first and foremost their family home.

A paneled front door opens onto the entrance hall, formerly a breezeway, furnished with an English highboy and Chippendale-style chairs. The portrait is of the current owner, Joseph Gee III.

FLEUR DE LYS
HOLLY SPRINGS, MISSISSIPPI

*The handsome redbrick façade of Fleur de Lys, dating from
the mid-1830s, bears an architectural reference to Albemarle County, Virginia,
where the original owners came from.*

Holly Springs is a small, pretty town with a splendid selection of antebellum houses and churches. Before the Civil War, Holly Springs was one of the largest and most prosperous cities in the state of Mississippi. It was settled in large part by Virginians and Carolinians, which explains its quality of elegance and sophistication. The fashionable architectural genres of the period are handsomely represented—Gothic Revival, Greek Revival, and Georgian styles delight the eye as one walks the city streets. Its fame may not be as widespread as that of Natchez to the south or Madison, Georgia, to the east, but that is probably because most of the houses in Holly Springs are private, and therefore off-limits to tourists— except once a year, on the annual spring tour.

The table in the front hall is one of a pair of card tables.
The gilt mirror is in the art nouveau style. The chairs are nineteenth-century
walnut, with needlepoint covers made by Harriett Tyson's stepmother.
The photograph is of Harriett, aged five.

In 1860 Holly Springs became an important link on the Mississippi Railroad to New Orleans, and in 1862 General Ulysses S. Grant made the town his supply base during his campaign against Vicksburg. When his wife, Julia, came to visit, they set up house at Walter Place, a Greek Revival mansion built in 1859 by a lawyer for his wife and ten children.

When the Confederate general Earl Van Dorn and his cavalry raided Holly Springs in December 1862, he told his men not to enter Walter Place as long as Julia Grant remained inside. Grant meanwhile, surprised by the rebel attack, had to withdraw temporarily from Holly Springs into Tennessee. In spite of this setback, Grant appreciated the enemy general's thoughtfulness toward Julia, and when he returned to Holly Springs, he forbade his own troops to occupy Walter Place, thus saving the house from destruction.

In most cases, however, it was Southern women themselves who came to the rescue, such as the female population of Holly Springs who so successfully charmed the Union army preparing to torch the town that the soldiers found themselves unable to complete their destructive task.

Fleur de Lys was not a major player in the Civil War. It was built by the Burton family in 1840. Marjorie Harriett Tyson, the present owner, inherited the house from her father, whose first wife was a Burton. "My maternal great-grandfather, Robert Alexander, was the first white man born in this county," says Harriett Tyson. The Burtons and the Alexanders were friends in Albemarle County, Virginia, before coming to Marshall County in the late 1830s.

ABOVE AND OPPOSITE: *In the dining room, the chandelier is modern, as are the lace table linens. The highly ornamented sideboard and chairs were made in English oak by R. J. Horner, the nineteenth-century New York cabinetmaker. The silver candlesticks are by Buccellati, and the family china is kept in a walnut cabinet in the hall outside the dining room.*

John Shields Burton and his wife, Mary Malvina, began to build Fleur de Lys after their arrival in the county, but ten years later they divorced, with the house unfinished and with Mary Malvina left to rear her children alone.

In the early twentieth century Mary Malvina's granddaughter Mary Burton married Harriett's father, Robert Tyson, who was thirty years younger than his wife, a very unusual age difference, even in those days. "Mary Burton Tyson was my father's mother's age—he was twenty-seven and she was fifty-seven. And rich," adds his daughter. The family continued to live in Fleur de Lys, which had been completed after John and Mary Malvina's divorce. It remains a handsome middle Virginia-style mansion, its architecture making reference to Albemarle County, Virginia, where the Burtons originally came from. Designed in a T shape, it has internal and external brick walls, a four-columned portico, and what were originally tin-roofed porches. The porches have since been adapted to create a kitchen and bath on one side of the T, and a sunroom on the other. Most of the details of the house are still in their original state. The eighteen original windows upstairs and down have English sashes outside and French glass window closures inside.

Much of the land that surrounded the house was sold or given away before the Civil War, and it now stands on four acres. The wrought-iron railings with their fleur-de-lys finials (hence the name of the house) elegantly define the perimeter of the property. Before the Civil War, there was an iron foundry in Holly Springs which naturally became a target for the Union Army, who destroyed it. The fence, testament to the skill of

The parlor fireplace is original. The case clock is mahogany, brought by covered wagon from Virginia in the 1840s. The furniture came from France and was shipped from New Orleans by rail to the house. The gilt mirror frame is currently lacking the mirror.

TOP: *In the downstairs bedroom, the two marble bookends in the form of heads of pointers ("bird dogs") belonged to Harriett's father, Robert Tyson.* ABOVE: *The English oak sideboard with caryatids is typical of R.J. Horner's ornate cabinetry.* OPPOSITE: *The Empire bed in the master bedroom is mahogany, as is the bedside table with caryatids. The floors are heart pine, and like the windows, are original to the house.*

the nineteenth-century iron workers, had originally been placed in front of the courthouse, and thence was acquired in 1932 by Harriett's father.

The interior of the house retains the flavor of its nineteenth-century origins. The floors are heart pine, and the coal-burning fireplaces are original. Much of the furniture came from France and England to New Orleans and was shipped up by rail to Holly Springs. Harriett Tyson's fine Empire bed has a particular claim to fame. The Burtons were friends of Sam Houston, the Virginia-born soldier and politician who became governor of Texas in 1859 after having been governor of Tennessee. "He often used to stay here in his commutations between Washington to the Brazos and back," she explains. "He slept in my bed!"

Harriett Tyson lived for twenty years in New York City, returning home after having been awarded the property and other real estate, as the only child of Robert Tyson, in a trust litigation between herself and her stepmother's heirs. She obtained possession of Fleur de Lys in 1985. Her experience of moving from the South to the North and back again gives her an unusual perspective on her dual identities. "Most people who partake of American culture tend to take one side or the other. I have had the enriching experience of living in rather intense milieus both in the North and the South." Surrounded by six bassett hounds, which she breeds, she now seems fully reconciled to her Southern roots. "Living in Holly Springs in these historically unique circumstances is a most worthy experiment," she says simply.

THE ELMS
NATCHEZ, MISSISSIPPI

*An unusual plant stand made of
tree roots decorates the porch overlooking the garden.*

Like many Southern houses, the Elms has grown and flowered from very long-lived roots. The original house was built by John Henderson, a well-educated Scottish Presbyterian settler whose family arrived in Natchez in 1787 and whose claim to (considerable) fame was that he wrote the first book printed in the region, on the subject of Thomas Paine. Although the oldest part of the house therefore probably dates from the 1780s, examination of the floorboards and other architectural details date the front and back porches and small parlor to 1804. The original building was a two-and-a-half story brick house with two rooms on each floor. Its architecture reveals a Spanish influence, with low ceilings, wide verandas, and thick walls. When the house was built, its location was almost out of town, which meant that the owners were able to acquire, along with the house, 114 acres of fertile land.

The original two-story façade of The Elms, dating from 1804, with columns and verandas, is glimpsed rising above a green landscape.

From 1825 to 1835, the house was inhabited by Reverend and Mrs. George Potts, who turned it into a Presbyterian rectory (no doubt the original owner would have been pleased), adding a formal parlor and master bedroom. During this time, those 114 acres were transformed into a magnificent garden. The mid-nineteenth-century author Joseph Holt Ingraham, traveling past the Elms during the Potts's tenure, was struck by the beauty of the landscape: "Clumps of foliage, of the deepest green, were enameled with flowers of the brightest hues, and every tree was an aviary."

In the 1850s the house was sold to David Stanton, an important merchant and cotton dealer in Natchez. David Stanton's taste did not stretch to pretentious architecture. Rather than build a new house, he added a two-story wing to the Elms in the Greek revival style, with second- and third-floor galleries guarded by wooden balustrades. He changed the position of the front entrance of the house from south to west and added a billiard hall in the side yard (now annexed to another Greek Revival mansion next door). He also enclosed the original front porch to serve as the front hall. In so doing he included the handsome cast-iron staircase (the only one of its kind in Mississippi) that had been part of the exterior of the house, thereby transforming it into a dramatic inner staircase up to the new second floor. Stanton also refitted the old wooden mantels in Carrara marble and added doors with stained glass.

Thanks to his ingenious extensions, the house became much more spacious, although constantly referring back to its idiosyncratic architectural history. The blending of the old and

OPPOSITE: *The piano in the little sitting room is by John Adams of Louisville, Kentucky, and was brought to the house by the owner's great-grandmother for her two daughters. The portrait is of Alma Carpenter, aged eighteen, by Igor Pantuhoff.* BELOW: *A statue in the garden provides a charming reminder of what was once considered one of the most beautiful gardens in Natchez.*

ABOVE: *The tiara and scepter belong to Mrs. Carpenter's daughter who was Natchez Pilgrimage Queen in 1966. Behind is a picture of Alma Carpenter in 1946 when she was Queen.* OPPOSITE: *The hall was originally the front porch of the old house. When it was enclosed by previous owner David Stanton in 1858, the lacy cast-iron outdoor staircase was adapted as access to the second floor. The Rococo Revival parlor set was brought to The Elms by the Drake family in 1869.*

new additions gives the house its special personality. Uneven floors, high and low ceilings, the exposure of what was once an exterior wall in the breakfast room, along with slave bells that had once been on the back porch, tell the story of the house's history as much as the furniture and portraits.

It is an interesting aspect of Natchez history that while David Stanton was making his additions, his brother Frederick had just built his own family home in the center of town. Unlike The Elms with its quirky charm, Stanton Hall, completed in 1857, is a massive Greek Revival–Georgian palace, one of the largest and most imposing mansions in the South. The two brothers clearly had very different ideas of architecture— and their own position in society. Both the Stanton brothers were collectors; some of David Stanton's acquisitions were shared with his brother, who had the more challenging task of furnishing his far bigger mansion down the street.

Unlike the familiar and painful Civil War stories that so often swirl around these houses, a highly romantic tale attaches to The Elms during the four-year-long engagement between 1861 and 1865. All the Stanton men went off to fight, leaving behind the ladies of the house. When Natchez was occupied by the Union soldiers, General Walter Q. Gresham became concerned about the safety of David Stanton's mother, wife, and their fifteen-year-old niece, Nannie Thornhill, since the house was so far on the outskirts of town. "We [were] furnished a guard at night of two soldiers," recalled Nannie Thornhill later. "One was an old man, the other a young soldier of 22. Early evenings until bedtime they played cards and

RIGHT: *The attic was completed as a bedroom. The original plaster on the walls is still smooth as glass. The mantel has a stippled effect. The sconce originally burned coal gas.* OPPOSITE: *In the attic, a collection of hoop skirts are hung on a rack, along with a World War I helmet picked up by Alma Carpenter's father when serving as an enlisted man in France.*

had music with us and then stood guard until sunrise." When the regiment was summoned to leave Natchez and report to Vicksburg, the Stanton household was thrown into consternation. "Grandmother did not know what to do, but on my insistence she concluded to call on General Gresham, whom we had never met." The general agreed to leave one soldier behind as a guard, first selecting the old man, since the younger one would be better able to endure the long march to Vicksburg. But the charming fifteen-year-old was so persuasive in her objections that the general agreed that they should draw straws as to who should stay behind. "I did so and we got the younger soldier!"

In a romantic denouement, Miss Thornhill later married the soldier, whose name was Lieutenant W. P. Callon of the Fourth Illinois Infantry, and whose career led him to an important position as member of the bar of central Illinois. After his death, Mrs. Callon returned home to Natchez, but, as author Matilda Gresham tartly noted, "Though eligible and of the bluest Southern blood, she is not one of the 'Daughters'"

(the United Daughters of the Confederacy). Of course not. She had married a Yankee!

In 1878 Mosley John Posey Drake and his wife, Caroline, bought The Elms after renting it for a while, and their great-granddaughter Alma Kellogg Carpenter now lives here. The Drake family, whose early ancestors included a Revolutionary War soldier and a Methodist minister, brought their own treasures to the house, such as a set of Rococo Revival parlor furniture that still retains its original wool plush upholstery, and delightful framed designs of embroidery, wax flowers and fruit, made by Alma Carpenter's great-aunt, Alma Drake.

Alma Carpenter's family maintained the beautiful gardens so admired by the nineteenth-century traveler, and she recalls that the grounds used to be big enough to contain a tennis court, where summertime matches were popular social events. Now the town has spread outward and all but enveloped The Elms, along with most of its land. However, the garden retains its power with the boxwood lining the paths and azaleas, camellias, wisteria, and flowering shrubs still blooming in the shade of the great live oaks. A privy and slave quarters nestle in a distant corner, and the latticed gazebo remains a pleasing focal point. If there is a somewhat unceremonious feeling to the overall view these days, Alma Carpenter, who has lived here all her life, is not complaining. "I don't like the garden to look manicured," she says firmly. "In the old days, no one had lawn mowers. The grass was sickled." Sitting on the old back porch, or upstairs on one of the galleries, she surveys her wild and wonderful garden with satisfaction.

ABOVE: *The dining-room window originally opened onto the front porch; it's now enclosed and serving as the entrance hall.* OPPOSITE TOP LEFT: *The formal parlor has a coal-burning fireplace, with a Carrara marble mantel.* OPPOSITE TOP RIGHT: *The dining room table belonged to Alma Carpenter's mother, and the china was made by John Ridgeway, circa 1840.* OPPOSITE BOTTOM: *On the walls of the den are family portraits and a copy of a portrait of Beatrice Cenci by Guido Reni.*

GREEN LEAVES
NATCHEZ, MISSISSIPPI

The front parlor, separated from the back parlor by original, heavy velvet
curtains hanging from pocket doors, contains Rococo Revival rosewood furniture
(reupholstered). The wallpaper dates from 1849. The wood in both parlors
is cypress and was originally painted white except for a portion of the
pocket doors painted to look like oak.

The historical importance of this house is indicated by its position on half a city block at the southeast end of old Natchez. Its evocative name is inspired by the enormous live oak trees that shade the house, one of which is four hundred years old. The earliest house on this site dates from 1804. The present house, a charming one-story raised cottage, was built by architect E. P. Fourniquet in 1838. In 1849, George Washington Koontz, who had come to Natchez in 1836 as a twenty-year-old from Pennsylvania and become a successful banker, bought the house. "Natchez was the place to be," declares his great-granddaughter, Virginia Beltzhoover Morrison, who lives in the house and is caretaker of its heritage.

Virginia Morrison's grandmother was married in the back parlor, with its set of mahogany Rococo Revival furniture. At the far end is a bookcase, containing, along with the books, a collection of fans, satin shoes, and teacups.

In 1845 George W. Koontz married Mary Roane Beltzhoover, whose family had also come to Natchez from Pennsylvania in 1832. By the time they moved into Green Leaves, he had become partner with William Britton in a thriving bank. He added a wing with three bedrooms to the house for his growing family, which, at final count, consisted of eight children. He also extended the gallery and gardens to accommodate this large brood.

During the Civil War, Mr. Koontz traveled to Europe to negotiate loans for the Confederate army, and he became a trusted friend of Jefferson Davis. In spite of this very public alliance, Green Leaves escaped the ravages of many of its neighbors during and after the war. The Britton & Koontz Bank was closed by Federal troops after they arrived in Natchez, but President Andrew Johnson signed a pardon for both bankers, and the bank was quickly reinstated when the war ended. The one surviving reminder of those troubled times is a bullet hole in the transom of the front door of the house, fired at Mr. Koontz by a carpetbagger during Reconstruction.

Right in the middle of the Civil War, in 1862, the Koontzes produced a daughter, who was named Virginia Lee both for their beleaguered Confederate leader and the state of Virginia. That year, most inhabitants of Natchez moved out when the gunboat *Essex* shelled the town. Luckily, the Koontzes were able to keep their family together. In 1891 Virginia Lee married her cousin Melchior Stewart Beltzhoover, who had spent most of his childhood in Europe, only returning to the South when he was twenty-one years old. The marriage took place at

TOP LEFT: *Porcelain figures and family photographs rest amicably on a table.* TOP RIGHT: *A mahogany glass-doored cabinet in the hall is crammed with heirlooms, ornaments, and toys.* BOTTOM LEFT: *In the front parlor, next to a cabinet filled with Confederate mementoes, is a portrait of Seargent Prentiss, a Whig politician known as the "silver-tongued orator of the South."* BOTTOM RIGHT: *In the back parlor, an ornately carved glass-doored bookcase, identical to that in the front parlor, holds, among other treasures, Victorian jewelry made out of human hair.*

Green Leaves. Their son, another Melchior, was born in the house in 1892, and in 1917 he married Ruth Audley Britton Wheeler, a descendant of the Britton who had been the banking partner of George W. Koontz. Melchior and Ruth Audley were the parents of three children, one of whom, Virginia, still lives at Green Leaves. Thus Southerners seem always to have stayed close to one another, accumulating ties of kinship in a way that ultimately becomes almost impossible to unravel, and thus the family house remains the center of births, marriages, and deaths through the generations.

Green Leaves is a worthy upholder of these traditions. Its architecture, position, and size reflect a security and longevity that are increasingly rare in this country of social and economic mobility. Its design is a fine example of local 1840s architecture. Unabashedly Greek Revival, the front façade of the house boasts an impressively large portico with a heavily decorated entablature, from which a steep flight of steps leads down toward the street. The rear of the house is less formal, with a long gallery punctuated by tall white columns. A simple staircase leads to a pathway, lined with boxwood, into the charming formal backyard garden shaded by an ancient live oak tree.

The interior of Green Leaves is equally expressive, vividly reflecting the taste of a prosperous Southern family before the Civil War. The marble fireplaces are from Italy; Empire furniture represents the European style of the period; English and early American silver shimmers on the dining-room table, along with a set of bird china attributed to John James

ABOVE: *The round table is a poker table from the nineteenth-century steamboat the Robert E. Lee.*
OPPOSITE TOP LEFT: *The wallpaper in the hall is a reproduction of a Williamsburg design dating from 1849. The large portrait above it is of Melchior R. Beltzhoover and his sister, Roane, painted in 1905 by New York artist William Thorne.* OPPOSITE TOP RIGHT: *In the dining room, the mahogany dining table displays silver, some English, some American, the wedding presents of five generations of the family. The cane seats on the chairs are said to be cooler than upholstery. The sideboard is mahogany, and the still life of flowers and fruit above it was painted in 1836 and signed by A. Chakel.* OPPOSITE BOTTOM: *In the game room, the large cabinet contains china attributed to Audubon. There were five hundred pieces in the original set.*

ABOVE: *The bedroom has a mahogany Empire tester bed, with a daybed at its foot. The wallpaper dates from the late nineteenth or early twentieth century. The portrait is of Virginia Morrison's great-grandmother Eliza McCrery Britton.* OPPOSITE: *Built in 1838, this town house represents classic Greek Revival architecture of the period, with columns, a pedimented portico, and a low roof line. It has been occupied by the Koontz family and their descendants since 1849.*

Audubon. The wallpaper and carpet in the front parlor are original, as are the gilt valances, dating from 1849. Some of the curtain fabrics have been replaced, and chairs and sofas are reupholstered, but the feeling is timeless. Family portraits in every room remind the visitor of the generational connection that goes back over 150 years.

Bookcases and glass-doored cabinets are all filled with mementoes—a great-grandmother's china cups, old wedding fans, satin shoes, unusual jewelry made out of human hair (a popular custom in Victorian times), scent bottles, and books. "I'd love to get behind all this and have a look at all the books," says Virginia Morrison, sighing at the impossible task of burrowing past the clutter of faded treasures. A particularly interesting item is the French sword bestowed on Colonel Daniel Beltzhoover during the Vicksburg campaign by a dying Englishman, who said as he expired that it had been used in the Battle of Waterloo in 1815.

"The house has been lived in by the same family for so long that we have almost everything anyone could possibly want to see," says Virginia Morrison, who opens the house during the spring and fall Pilgrimage. "I say to visitors, 'Just tell me what you're interested in and it's probably here at Green Leaves.'"

LANSDOWNE
NATCHEZ, MISSISSIPPI

The attic at Lansdowne contains a collection of old family possessions
dating back more than a century: steamer trucks, vases, books, a child's sleigh,
a spinning wheel, a baby carriage, and a broken cradle.

Most of the antebellum houses in Natchez are townhouses in the truest sense of the word, built by plantation owners as an urban alternative to country life or by business and professional families working in the city. Lansdowne, however, is situated quite a distance from the center of Natchez and was originally a working plantation house surrounded by eight hundred acres for growing cotton and livestock. The land was given in 1852 as a wedding present from David Hunt, one of the richest men in Mississippi, to his daughter Charlotte. She and her husband, George M. Marshall, built on the property a splendid Greek Revival and Georgian mansion that was finished a year later. They named it Lansdowne in honor of their aristocratic English friend, the Marquis of Lansdowne. "There were larger plantations in Louisiana," says the Marshalls' great-granddaughter, Mrs. Devereux Slatter, who lives at Lansdowne with her brother, George M. Marshall IV. "But Natchez had its share. The town was extremely prosperous and had the advantage of the fact that the Mississippi never overflowed its banks on our side of the river."

The exterior of Lansdowne has a painted brick façade, green shutters, and an elaborate widow's walk. It was originally planned as a two-story house, evidenced by the unusually tall chimneys.

The house, built of brick and painted a delicate peach with green shutters, has only one story, although according to the Marshalls, "our great grandparents had planned to put on a second floor. The chimneys have double flues." (The plans were never completed owing to the disruptions of the Civil War and later financial downturns.) The modest exterior of Lansdowne belies its size. The front façade consists of a four-columned portico and large pediment, with the extra-tall chimneys punctuating the roofline. Inside, the space is dramatic. The hall, which stretches through the center of the house to the back courtyard, is sixty-five feet long ("great for parties," note the owners). There is a large parlor and dining room in the front, with bedrooms in the rear. At the back of the house, separate from the main building, are brick outhouses that were once kitchens, a school room, slave quarters, and a billiard room. Farther away, toward a stream and fine stands of shade trees in the back of the property, is a full-scale walk-in dollhouse, built by George Marshall III for his only daughter. "He thought I wanted somewhere of my own to play," she remembers.

The first Marshalls had seven children, but only three grew to maturity, the others succumbing to diseases common to the area, such as dysentery, yellow fever, malaria, diphtheria, and typhoid. (The climate presented a permanent threat to Southern families.) George Marshall was a political activist, and by the time the Civil War broke out he had become an ardent secessionist. He fought in the war for a short time and was wounded in the leg at Shiloh. Shortly afterward, he paid

In the garden sits a life-size dollhouse, built by George Marshall III for his only daughter, Devereux, then about eight years old. Inside is a perfectly furnished bed-sitting room, with a table set for tea and twin beds. Even the pictures on the wall and the toys on the shelves are perfectly proportioned for a little girl.

ABOVE: The hall of Lansdowne is a spectacular sixty-five feet long, ideal for parties. The furniture is French, English, and American, mostly oak and mahogany. The floors are heart pine. OPPOSITE: The parlor is dominated by a set of French rosewood furniture and an Aubusson carpet. The fireplace and baseboards are faux marble. The rich, deep-pink curtains are copies of the original, matched to the wallpaper, with valances made of gilded plaster.

ABOVE: In the dining room, the lovely wallpaper is a copy of Zuber's 1850s design. The table and chairs were inherited from the family. LEFT: The mahogany sideboard, original to the house, displays mostly American family silver, with a few English pieces. The portrait of the Marshalls's great-great grandfather was painted by one of the most popular artists of the period, Thomas Sully. OPPOSITE: This bedroom was once the library. The mahogany tester bed came from New Orleans. In the center of a wall of family pictures is a photograph of George M. Marshall III, the present owner's father.

At the center of the long hall
is a glass-fronted oak cupboard
filled with books. The portrait
above the Elizabethan chair is of
the Duchess of Portsmouth.

someone else to continue fighting on his behalf. In one of the
painful ironies of the Civil War, Marshall's father was against
the war and spent time with the Union's General Grant, in
hopes of saving the South's cotton business. This was not
unusual, according to the Marshalls. "Natchez was a divided
city and anxious to hold on to its fortunes. There were many
here who made connections with Northerners and even
invested in the North in anticipation of losing the war."

On December 12, 1865, with Natchez under Federal occupa-
tion, Lansdowne was broken into by eleven Union soldiers.
The family was held at gunpoint in a bedroom, and Charlotte
was knocked to the floor because she refused to hand over the
closet keys. This bold stand was not forgiven. When the soldiers left, it is said they broke the family's French apricot heirloom china into pieces and scattered the shards along the road

that led out of the estate. The story also goes that the Marshalls' butler, Robert, had hidden most of the family silver under the parlor floor. In recognition of his lifetime of service, both he and his wife, Susan, were buried in 1918 in the Marshall family cemetery.

The interior of Lansdowne is a hymn to its early prosperity. Fine examples of French, English, and American furniture fill the rooms, with family portraits and many original curtain and upholstery fabrics. Perhaps the most spectacular aspect of Lansdowne's interiors is its wall decoration. In the parlor, the wallpaper, which is original to the house, was designed by the famous nineteenth-century French artist Jean Zuber. Its Rococo Revival pattern, in soft, muted colors, adds great elegance to the room. In the dining room the charming floral wallpaper is a copy of an original Zuber design, enhancing the

fine collections of silver and porcelain on display on sideboards and glass-fronted cabinets. In case there was any doubt about Southern families never throwing anything away, both the cellar and the attic of Lansdowne are stuffed with family treasures, ranging from old glass wine bottles, steamer trunks, and sidesaddles to spinning wheels and horse skulls.

The gardens of Lansdowne are wild and beautiful, with live oaks drooping over overgrown paths as though weighed down by their Spanish moss. One of these paths leads to the family cemetery, a small piece of land surrounded by a low wall, filled with gravestones, most of which are still clearly decipherable. They include the infants lost to the first Marshalls who lived here. ("Coralee aged 10 months, 2 days; Maria, aged 10 months 4 days; Catherine aged 4 years, 1 month and 23 days.") There are the graves of other relatives and of Robert and Susan, the Marshalls' loyal servants. "My great-grandparents, grandparents, parents, and aunt Agnes, are buried here," says George M. Marshall IV, looking down at the poignant markers. The implication of his own rightful place here among his forebears remains unspoken. "The extent to which family history is retained is related to how long the family has stayed in the same place," George Marshall declares quietly. This cemetery, perhaps more than anywhere else in Natchez or indeed anywhere in the South, speaks of the long, unbroken line between generations, and of the earth to which they are all ultimately returned.

TOP: *Finials, a horse skull, and pieces of glass and pottery are reminders of Lansdowne's history.* ABOVE: *The portrait of "Miss Agnes Marshall," owner of this steamer trunk, hangs in the hall.* OPPOSITE: *This is the Marshalls's great-grandmother's wine cellar, now stocked only with bottles. The white finials are copies of the originals on the roof of the house.*

LOUISIANA

*The South is a very big place, yet there is hardly
a district that didn't have its skirmish, its federal gunboat
sunk in a bayou—where some old-timer won't tell you,
"Yes, they came through here." Its startling to realize that there
were more casualties in the Civil War than in all
the American forces of World War II, and more
than in all other American wars put together.*

—WALKER PERCY, "LIFE IN THE SOUTH"

CATALPA
ST. FRANCISVILLE, LOUISIANA

*Catalpa Plantation, with its charming one-story columned
façade, dormers, and porch that runs the width of the house, is shaded
by live oaks festooned with Spanish moss.*

By 1850 roughly two-thirds of America's millionaires were planters living along the Mississippi River between Natchez and New Orleans. St. Francisville in West Feliciana Parish, a small town growing up on the banks of the river between these two great cities, soon became transformed from a boat landing for French and Spanish missionaries into the largest port in the region, transporting cotton, sugar, and tobacco throughout the United States and to the rest of the world. Although settled first by the French, by the 1800s the English soon outnumbered them, and St. Francisville became known as English Plantation Country. Thanks to its explosive commercial success, some of the finest houses in the South were built here.

The portrait above the mantel in the dining room is of James P. Bowman, painted by Jacques Amans. The sideboard was made by French cabinet-maker Prudent Francis Mallard. The mantel, like those in the rest of the house, is made of cast iron and painted to look like marble—a typical stylistic characteristic of the period.

Catalpa is one of the few that is owned and lived in by the descendants of the original builder. His name was William Fort, and he came to West Feliciana Parish from North Carolina in the late 1700s, having heard of the potential of the land in this part of Louisiana. The date of the original house is thought to be as early as 1800. A raised cottage built of brick, typical of the period, it was extremely simple in design, with the living and bedrooms on one floor and an enclosed porch at the rear. Live oaks planted in the garden date from 1814. According to Mary Thompson, the surviving member of the Fort family now living here, the house's name, Catalpa, was inspired by the tree, although there are none here now.

By the 1850s Catalpa had become a thriving cotton and sugar plantation under the guidance of William Fort's son, William Johnston Fort. The house became a repository of much fine furniture, including a Pleyel piano, dated 1848, which Mrs. Fort played so often (although she later became blind) that she wore down the keys. She also loved flowers, and it is clear that the second Mr. Fort shared this passion. All types of shrubs and plants were planted on the thirty-acre estate, and a greenhouse was filled with orange and banana trees, vines and tropical flowers. He created a lake, with swans and a fountain. He designed a park with peacocks, pigeon houses, and scented plants and flowers. There were orchards and vegetable gardens. He also had the original notion of lining the elliptical-shaped avenue leading to the house with large pink-lined conch shells, some of which still remain in the front yard of the house.

ABOVE: *The portrait in the dining room of William Turnbull, who drowned at the age of twenty-eight, is a Thomas Sully copy. On the marble-topped table is a collection of French fruit dishes decorated in Napoleon green.* OPPOSITE: *The dining room, with pocket doors opening into the parlor, has an eighteenth-century mahogany dining table and chairs. The silver service was made for the family with the Turnbull monogram on the tray. The silver centerpiece was made at Tiffany's to represent the trunk of a live oak.*

RIGHT: *Above a charming curved-fronted, marble-topped washstand hangs a pair of eighteenth-century prints.* BELOW: *In the parlor, a collection of Victorian portraits is displayed on an inlaid tabletop flanked by two ornate candlesticks.* OPPOSITE: *The front bedroom, like all the bedrooms, is situated on the ground floor. It has a rosewood half-tester bed and dresser made by Mallard. Over the mantel, on which stand two Venetian glass vases, is a portrait of Eliza Pirrie of Oakley Plantation, Mary Thompson's great-great-grandmother. It is attributed to Audubon.*

ABOVE: *One of the portraits in the front hall is of Mary Thompson's great-grandfather James Bowman.* OPPOSITE: *In the parlor, the rosewood furniture was made by Mallard between 1820 and 1835. The portrait over the mantel is of Sarah Turnbull, of Rosedown Plantation, great-grandmother of Catalpa's owner. It was painted by Thomas Sully.*

However, its beauty was not to last. The Civil War dealt a harsh hand to Catalpa. William Johnston Fort died shortly after the war began, leaving a widow and seven children. When the Union army reached St. Francisville, the house was requisitioned. The soldiers in the area seem to have been unusually destructive, ravaging the greenhouse and much of the gardens and uprooting plants and shrubs while the slaves fled. (In the house today are reminders of that time—a silver butter dish and coffee pot, both dented from having been buried in the pond to hide them from the invaders.) As was the case so often during this bitter conflict, Mrs. Fort refused to abandon the house and continued to raise her children there after the war was over. Her fortitude, like that of so many Southern women during those years, allowed Catalpa to remain in the family to this day.

Almost forty years after the war, another tragic event overtook Catalpa. During the long, humid Southern summers, it was customary to stuff chimneys with rags and leaves to prevent birds from settling there. "Unfortunately, in a sudden cold spell in October 1900," Mary Thompson tells the story, "while the men of the house were out hunting, my great-grandmother, a little forgetful, decided to light a fire." The chimney went up in flames and with it the building. However, the fire was slow burning, and almost everything inside the house was saved, though the house would have to be rebuilt.

A year later a local newspaper announced the housewarming of the new Catalpa. It was built, like its predecessor, on one floor (except for second-floor attics). The architecture this

time, reflecting contemporary taste, was in the Victorian bungalow style, with delicate columns and balustrades surrounding a generous front porch. Today the house seems comfortable with its dual past, still shaded by the same live oaks, now almost two hundred years old, and still guarded by two iron greyhounds, brought from England for the first Catalpa, one with a hole in its back made by a Union soldier's musket in a heedless gesture of farewell.

The interior of Catalpa, thanks to its rescue from the fire, is a hymn to old Southern kinship. Mary's great-grandparents were Sarah Turnbull and James Bowman. The Turnbulls came from Rosedown, a plantation a few miles from Catalpa. The Bowmans came from Oakley, another plantation in West Feliciana Parish, made famous as the temporary home of the great artist John James Audubon. (He was employed as a tutor there from 1821 to 1830.) The merger of these two families brought riches to Catalpa in the form of furniture, paintings, silver, and decorative objects, and when Rosedown was sold out of the family in the 1950s, Catalpa was again the beneficiary.

In fact, there is very little in this house that does not have a direct family provenance. There are portraits of the Turnbulls and the Bowmans, family china and silver dating from the mid-1800s, baby carriages, even a cobalt blue perfume bottle belonging to Sarah Turnbull. Her great-granddaughter is now the caretaker of these treasures. "I sometimes feel my ancestors are still alive," Mary Thompson says. "So much of their world surrounds me here at Catalpa."

The exterior of Catalpa, shaded by live oaks hung with Spanish moss, is guarded by two iron greyhounds brought to the house from England, one with a bullet hole in its back, the parting shot of a Union soldier.

TENNESSEE

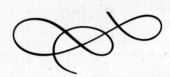

Once or twice, in the summer [my grandmother] took
us to South Pittsburgh, Tennessee, to visit the Ralstons, about
which I remember honey kept in a barrel on the back porch, hot
sun on pine needles, and the wildness and beauty of my
grandmother's nephew, young Preston Faller Jr., whistling as
he dressed for a dance in a room that contains in my memory only
a glittering brass bed and roses on the wallpaper and dusk
turning violet at the open windows.

—TENNESSEE WILLIAMS, "GRAND"

FAIRVUE
GALLATIN, TENNESSEE

*A delicate lace curtain protects a room from too much sunlight
while allowing the breezes to flow freely.*

Gallatin is in Sumner County,
which was settled by pioneers who came to the area in the 1700s. Land and workers were cheap, and several great plantation houses were built here over the years. Tennessee became a state in 1796, and six years later Gallatin (named for Albert Gallatin, Secretary of the Treasury under Presidents John Adams and Thomas Jefferson) came into existence as a town, twenty-five miles northeast of Nashville.

From Fairvue's portico, through the majestic iconic columns, the visitor beholds a wonderful view of the Tennessee landscape.

In 1832 a wealthy slave trader, Isaac Franklin, began to build Fairvue. The builder was David Morrison. Franklin already owned more than twenty thousand acres of land in Tennessee, Louisiana, and Texas, but he chose Gallatin as his home base, finding the area congenial and convenient, being close to the booming city of Nashville, the state's capital and home to two of the country's presidents, Andrew Jackson and James K. Polk.

The house, a two-story brick structure with Georgian and Greek Revival flourishes, is particularly imposing. Its east and west façades boast two-story pediments and four Ionic columns, each with porches and first-floor balustrades. Over the front door is a Georgian-style fanlight. Three high chimneys punctuate the gabled cedar-shingle roof, with a pair of dormer windows. The interior was equally grand, with Irish Kilkenny marble mantels and furnishings from New Orleans. When the house was built, a brick fence ran round the perimeter of the flower gardens and lawns, and as was the case with many important plantation houses, the buildings on the grounds provided most of Fairvue's infrastructure, including a smokehouse, barn, carriage house, blacksmith's shop, and extensive slave quarters.

In 1839 Isaac Franklin, then aged fifty, married Adelicia Hayes, daughter of a distinguished Nasvhille lawyer. She was twenty years old. It is said that when she first visited Fairvue, she wrote in the guest book, "I like this house and set my cap for its master." After the marriage, Franklin added a huge L-shaped wing on the south side of the house, which contains

ABOVE: *In the library, which Mrs. Wemyss calls the living room, is a particularly fine portrait of a family great-aunt attributed to Thomas Sully.*
OPPOSITE: *The hall of Fairvue, like many Southern houses of the period, has a central arch echoing the Palladian-style transom of the front door and rooms opening off it, allowing the breezes to flow through the house.*

ABOVE: The stable barn, once home to thoroughbred racehorses, retains its original overhanging roof providing a covered exercise track. LEFT: Extensive slave quarters were once a significant part of the Wemyss plantation. OPPOSITE TOP: The exterior façade of Fairvue, built in 1832, reflects the prosperity of its original owner with its two stories made of brick, Ionic columns, pediments, and dormers. OPPOSITE BOTTOM: This view of Fairvue shows the tall chimneys, double-height portico, and four Ionic columns that are a feature of both the east and west sides of the house.

the kitchen, breakfast room, and a circular staircase to the top floor. Although Franklin had a reputation for fairness, at the insistence of his Presbyterian abolitionist wife, he also gave up the slave trade.

Seven years after marrying this strong-minded and cultivated young woman, who was also a noted beauty, Franklin died, leaving Adelicia the house and plantation. After three years as a widow, Adelicia, now said to be one of the richest women in America, married Colonel Joseph Acklen, and they built Belmont Mansion in Nashville, an Italianate palace with extravagant gardens, statuary, and fountains. This lavish mansion was intended to be their summer home. Continuing what was beginning to look like a marital pattern, Adelicia's second husband also died prematurely, in 1863, leaving Adelicia sole owner of both Fairvue and Belmont.

Fairvue managed to escape the worst excesses of the Civil War, although many of the bloodiest engagements were fought close by, including the Battle of Stones River (fought from December 31, 1862 to January 2, 1863) and the Battle of Franklin (1864). Emerging relatively unscathed, and still in possession of vast tracts of land, Adelicia married her third husband, Dr. William Cheatham, in 1867. In so doing, she made him sign what would now be called a prenuptial agreement, in which he agreed that she would always retain ownership of her beautiful and valuable real estate. Adelicia outlived all her husbands and finally sold Fairvue to Charles Reed of New York in 1882. She died in New York in 1887 and is buried in the family vault in Nashville.

OPPOSITE TOP LEFT: *Family portraits, both old and new, are displayed on a table in the parlor.* OPPOSITE TOP RIGHT: *In the parlor, an original black Kilkenny mantel holds a classical marble urn and a pair of chandeliers; behind is a large nineteenth-century gilt mirror.* OPPOSITE BOTTOM: *The double parlor, with its rich, red rug original to the house, has a nineteenth-century Empire gilt mirror and family portraits. The black marble mantel was imported from Ireland.*

Charles Reed was a large, expansive character who was a well-known name in horse-breeding circles and who also had a penchant for gambling. He owned a string of famous race-horses and built grand stables for them at Fairvue, with an extended roof of slate from England forming a covered track that allowed the horses to exercise in any weather. He turned the grounds into paddocks and imported furniture said to be formerly owned by Marie Antoinette and Napoleon to fill the great rooms of the house, which became the center of many huge parties. Charles Reed retired from racing in 1902 and sold Fairvue in 1908, at which point it was passed down through a succession of owners. During the next twenty-six years the house suffered a severe decline; much of its interior was vandalized or destroyed.

In 1934, William H. Wemyss, cofounder of the General Shoe Corporation (now known as Genesco) bought Fairvue. When he acquired the house, the place was in sad repair. There were even chickens in the parlor. With the support of his family and the talent of local builders and craftsmen, he restored much of the original exterior architecture of Fairvue and brought it back to life. The brick fencing, for instance, that had been demolished during Charles Reed's ownership, was replaced in its original position as a frame for the garden. He also kept the stables and the covered track.

Work on the interior of Fairvue was equally thorough. The present decoration of the house, therefore, unlike many plantation houses of its kind, dates only from the time William Wemyss took over. In 1939 Ellen Stokes Wemyss, his second

ABOVE: A copy of a wallpaper by the French artist Zuber works as a fitting backdrop to a bronze statue of Napoleon. OPPOSITE: In a corner of the front hall of Fairvue, an Empire table holds an exceptional glass lamp with the Zuber scenic wallpaper decorating the wall behind it.

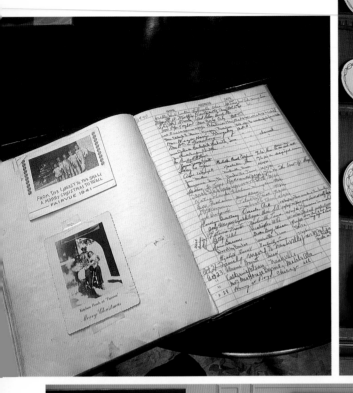

ABOVE: *The double parlor has a pair of matching rugs and copies of rosewood tufted furniture. Family portraits hang on the walls. The chandeliers came from the Hermitage Club in Nashville.* OPPOSITE TOP LEFT: *Diaries, notebooks, and photographs keep family history alive.* OPPOSITE TOP RIGHT: *A corner cabinet in the dining room displays china.* OPPOSITE BOTTOM: *The library of Fairvue, with red-painted niches for books and porcelain, has an Adam-style fireplace made of sycamore salvaged from a tree on the grounds dating from the eighteenth century.*

ABOVE: Portraits and photographs of family retainers share wall space in an informal corner of Fairvue. ABOVE RIGHT: The handmade brick wall was originally part of Fairvue's kitchens, built in 1832 and restored in 1939. The portraits are of Generals Lee and Longstreet. RIGHT: A fascinating sample of footwear, from ladies shoes to riding boots, is displayed in a cabinet, along with horse prints and crossed swords, in what was once part of Fairvue's extensive kitchens. OPPOSITE: The kitchen at Fairvue, with its marble-topped "biscuit-break."

LEFT: *A guest room at Fairvue, with twin mahogany beds and a copy of the original mantel.*
OPPOSITE: *The wide upper landing of Fairvue, lit by a window framed by a set of nineteenth-century prints.*

wife, embarked on a major restoration of the interior spaces, carefully replacing moldings and mantels and bringing in fine antiques. Some of the pieces are copies of the originals, as is the Jean Zuber wallpaper, but all were carefully selected to harmonize with the original architecture of the house. The success of these rooms, re-created in the twentieth century, proves the remarkable staying power of the decorating style of the old South.

Ellen Wemyss still lives at Fairvue. She is 106 years old and retains a strong grip on the household. Her large extended family sees that she is taken care of—just as this house, after all its vicissitudes, has also been taken care of and, astonishingly, survives.

GEORGIA

The floor was smooth and white, and the walls ceiled to the windows, the remainder being rough boards. The furniture was brought from the North and consisted of all those articles usually used in furnishing such rooms and looked very natural, all but my bed. This had very high posts and was covered with a spread so small that it gave the bed the appearance of standing on stilts!

EMILY BURKE, "PLEASURE AND PAIN: REMINISCENCES OF GEORGIA IN THE 1840S"

ST. ELMO
COLUMBUS, GEORGIA

On a table in the library with old leather-bound books
sits a photograph of Dr. and Mrs. Schley's daughter, Georgia,
taken at her debut in Columbus.

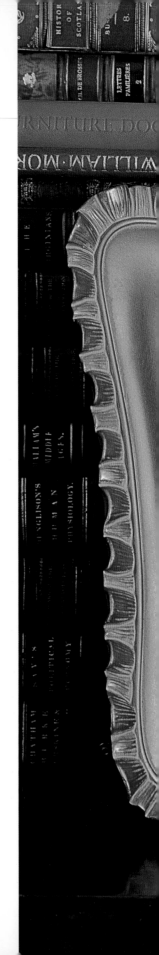

Perhaps the most famous house in
Southern fiction after Tara in *Gone with the Wind* is
St. Elmo, the mansion in Columbus, Georgia, where
Augusta Jane Evans Wilson wrote her novel of the
same name. In fact, when *St. Elmo* was published in
1866, it was almost as popular as the 1852 sensation
Uncle Tom's Cabin, and for many years continued to be
as wildly successful as *Gone with the Wind* later
became. The story now seems somewhat dated: A
rich upper-class Southerner called St. Elmo Murray
falls in love with Edna Earl, a young factory woman
with a dark past. Shamed by her background, she
spurns him. They are finally united at the end of the
book after Edna becomes a famous writer. Today
Scarlett O'Hara remains immortal whereas Miss Earl,
however famous her writing, has disappeared.
Still, the house, as is so often the case in the South,
retains its eloquence long after most of the characters
under its roof have become just memories.

A Regency portrait of a young girl, inherited from
Mrs. Schley's grandfather, hangs in the hall. On the mahogany table
are two English platters and a soup tureen.

Colonel Seaborn Jones, an important Georgia lawyer and legislator, broke ground on the house in 1828, and it was completed between 1831 and 1832. Originally the house was called Eldorado or simply the Old Jones Place. When Colonel Jones's daughter, Mary Howard, married Henry L. Benning, the fiery Confederate leader (after whom Fort Benning is named), they stayed on in her father's house and began to raise their family there. However, the aftermath of the Civil War proved particularly difficult for them. Marauders and thieving gangs threatened the area around St. Elmo so relentlessly that in the late 1860s the Bennings moved for safety's sake into downtown Columbus, where Henry Benning later died.

It was during the brief period before the Bennings forsook St. Elmo that the house played host to Augusta Jane Evans Wilson. Called the literary voice of the antebellum South, Augusta was born in Columbus in 1835. Her father, after suffering financial reverses that left him practically destitute by the end of the Civil War, was taken in by the Bennings (Augusta's mother was a relative), and after a year of living in the house, in 1866, the young author published the novel that transformed Eldorado into St. Elmo, the name of the house almost ever since. St. Elmo now contains a collection of memorabilia to Augusta Jane Evans Wilson, consisting of her autographed library, including first editions of all her novels, along with her desk and her silver tea urn and tray.

The house remained empty for several years after the departure of the Bennings and their famous cousin. In 1875 Captain and Mrs. James Slade purchased it and turned it into

OPPOSITE TOP LEFT: *A stuffed gazelle poses on a pile of antique volumes.* OPPOSITE TOP RIGHT: *The library's marble fireplace is original to the house. The heavy curtain fabric is forty years old.* OPPOSITE BOTTOM: *Light streams in from the French doors that open onto a balcony. A mahogany Sheraton bookcase against the left wall has been turned into a gun cabinet.*

ABOVE: *The set of portraits of Napoleon lining the staircase comes from the Fontaine family house, which has since been demolished.* OPPOSITE: *A staircase to the first-floor landing winds up from the hall. At its foot, an English glass-fronted china cabinet is packed with mementoes, including Oriental and English teacups, a Queen Anne punch ladle, a Georgian sand-timer, and a blue and white porcelain collection.*

a small boarding school for young ladies. The house changed hands again in 1940, when the Mobley family bought it, and the present owners, Dr. Philip and Mrs. Schley, moved in thirty-six years ago.

The name of the house is practically the only thing that has changed here over the years. Only four owners have inhabited St. Elmo since 1828, and although after the Civil War it was abandoned for a time, each new owner respected the history of the house and made careful, if any, alterations. Part of the reason for this conservatism was financial. Until recently, these families could not afford major reconstruction. "Like in Natchez, the old architecture survived because nobody had any money to do anything about it," observes Margot Schley. "We lived for five years in the house without air-conditioning. The only way people could keep cool in those days was by blowing a fan over bowls filled with blocks of ice in the rooms."

It is also worth noting that St. Elmo was built very solidly, proving remarkably resistant to decay. The house is raised off the ground by twelve sturdy columns one yard wide and forty feet high, thus keeping the building cool and preventing damp. The stucco walls are five bricks thick, the bricks handmade out of local clay. Local cedar trees were cut down for the decorative woodwork, and the floors are laid in heart pine. "The only wood that did not come from the property is the mahogany banister," says Philip Schley. The original plantation had over 350 acres, but like most agricultural estates close to towns in the Deep South, the property has diminished over

the years as suburban sprawl has devoured the landscape. However, the garden at St. Elmo still retains its beauty, thanks to fine old trees—oaks, elms, cedars—a brick dovecote, and filigree wrought-iron railings.

The wide front door opens into a hallway that runs the length of the house, bisected by an archway. The finely proportioned rooms on the ground floor speak of elegant parties and grand dinners, with chandeliers and marble fireplaces. Heavy pocket doors act as room dividers, separating the dining room from the parlor. An elegant curving staircase leads to the upstairs bedrooms, entered off a long landing, illuminated by an arched Palladian window and fanlight. The furniture and furnishings throughout the house come from both sides of the Schley family, showing their European antecedents—English Chippendale bureaus, French wallpaper, Scottish chests. Every room is filled with personal mementoes, even down to the bust of Jefferson given to Mrs. Schley by her husband for her birthday.

In 1997 the Schleys added a large conservatory onto the back of the house. Designed in perfect harmony with the original architecture, it has given them an airy and comfortable space to work, read, or entertain family. The most telling aspect of the addition, however, is that to their surprise, they found they could furnish this large new room almost entirely with what they had. "We hardly had to buy a thing," Margot Schley says, still amazed. "I had no idea how much furniture we had in the house."

The moral of this story is that old Southern families live

CLOCKWISE, FROM TOP LEFT: The second-floor balcony looks west over a small ornamental pool; the elaborate wrought-iron balustrade is original to the house. On the north side of the house, a bust of Jefferson (a birthday present to Margot Schley from her husband) is silhouetted in the window; the original balustrade had to be replaced. The side view of St. Elmo, with a wrought-iron fence that came from the Schley family supporting a curtain of ivy. A stone urn, filled with old doorknobs, is reflected in an old mirror stored in a corner under the house. The house is raised off the ground by columns, thus creating a shady patio below the first floor, accessed by a wooden staircase.

ABOVE: *Displayed on the piano are a silver candlestick and a silver-framed portrait of the Schleys's son, Philip, at West Point.* RIGHT: *The dining room is enlivened by an unusual French wallpaper that dates from the 1940s, as does the crystal chandelier. The sideboard and oversized mirror come from the Fontaines, a founding Columbus family who were antecedents of Mrs. Mobley, the last owner of the house before the Schleys. The mahogany table is English.* OPPOSITE: *The parlor fireplace is black Carrara marble. Hanging over it is a copy of Sir Joshua Reynolds's portrait of Nellie O'Brien (the original is in The Wallace Collection in London). The elegant curtains hang from wooden valances.*

with more stuff than even they could possibly imagine. But why should they ever part with anything? Augusta Jane Evans Wilson, after an impoverished upbringing, started to earn money from her novels but like many of her friends was crippled by the Civil War. When she saw her publisher in Mobile in the summer of 1865, he was distressed by her unstylish appearance and suggested she purchase some new attire. The author of *St. Elmo* replied, "Mr. Derby, my father has lost everything; the slaves have been freed, and all our property confiscated. I have no money with which to replenish my wardrobe." The message was not lost on later generations. As Margot Schley says, "It only goes to show how much clutter we are happy to live with."

STOKES-McHENRY HOUSE
MADISON, GEORGIA

*The two-story town house, built between 1820 and 1822,
reveals a charming mixture of Victorian and Greek Revival styles, in particular
the five-arched porch framed in ornately carved fretwork.*

Madison is one of Georgia's most picturesque cities. A nineteenth-century historian described it as "the most cultured and aristocratic town on the stagecoach route from Charleston to New Orleans." Its location is the key to its stylishness. Usefully situated in the center of communications between the eastern and western boundaries of the Deep South, and surrounded by hugely profitable cotton fields, from 1830 to 1860 it was a magnet for the local plantation owners. Eager to show off their wealth and sophisticated taste, they built elegant townhouses for their families in Madison in all the latest styles.

In the parlor, two mahogany Victorian chairs sit on each side of the fireplace, which was originally stained dark, as was the floor. The pastel portrait of the three McHenry children, including Dan Hicky's grandfather John McHenry, was painted in 1859.

So highly prized was this mecca of antebellum glory that when General William T. Sherman's Union army, under the command of General Henry Slocum, approached its borders after having devastated Atlanta sixty miles away, Georgia Senator Joshua Hill rode out with a delegation to meet the scorched-earth maestro's representative and plead Madison's cause. (Hill was an antisecessionist who had known Sherman's brother John in Washington when they were both serving in the U.S. Congress.) The result, mentioned in Sherman's memoirs, was that Senator Hill succeeded in saving the town from Sherman's wrath, a reprieve for which the townspeople and history are deeply grateful.

In a town filled with glorious Greek Revival, Italianate, and Victorian mansions, the Stokes-McHenry house has its own magic. Originally a modest lawyer's residence, with two rooms upstairs and two down, it was built between 1820 and 1822 for William S. Stokes, whose daughter married into the McHenry family, hence its double-barreled name. Both families were Scottish in origin. The first immigrant, James Hall McHenry, settled in Savannah and built a rather grand home there. He and his wife died young, leaving two orphan sons, the younger of whom, John Grieves McHenry, came to live and work in Madison. The McHenrys continued to live in the house, and by the time we reach the sixth generation, the torch has been passed to Dan Hicky, a retired fighter pilot, whose mother, Louise, was a McHenry. Slowed down now a little with vision loss, Dan writes a poem a week for the local newspaper, and with his wife, Hattie-Mina Reid Hicky, is

ABOVE: *A photograph of Hattie Mina Reid Hicky on her wedding day, April 27, 1944, is displayed on a table.* OPPOSITE: *In the children's room, a collection of Dan's grandmother's dolls, lovingly restored, are arranged with miniature furniture.*

RIGHT: In the dining room is a portrait of Beatrix, youngest daughter of Queen Victoria, thought to greatly resemble Dan Hicky's grandmother Zoe. The silver collection and chandelier are family heirlooms. BELOW: The library is in the oldest part of the house. The door opens into the hall. On the Chickering piano (circa 1840) is the sheet music of a song entitled "The Boys in Grey Are Growing Old." A handwritten music book is dated 1837. The ceiling lamp is quite old.

The parlor is a later addition dating from 1848–1852, with the original carpet.
The pressed brass valances were bought by Mr. Hicky's grandmother Zoe
in the early 1900s. The portrait is of Zoe, as is the marble bust beneath it.

keeper of the flame and passionate curator of this lovely old place.

The house is not the grandest in Madison, but its architecture reveals the prevailing taste—a mixture of Victorian and Greek revival styles, with a low-pitched roof and a charming porch with elaborately carved fretwork decorating the Victorian arches and supports. The front door is particularly interesting. Oversized, it was called a coffin door, being wide enough for coffins to pass through. Greek key and acanthus leaves are carved into its frame, with glass sidelights and transom.

Inside, the rooms reveal the evolution of the McHenry family. As the family became larger and more prosperous, between 1848 and 1852 the original layout of the ground floor was extended with the addition of a new parlor. The carpet in the parlor, now faded but still glowing in some places with its original colors, was bought in strips from a salesman and sewn together on the spot, since broadloom weave carpets as we know them were not yet in existence. Historic references abound. The secretary in the hall, for instance, is filled with letters dating back to the 1800s, and the drawers are lined not

with plastic or professional liner paper, but instead with 1860s newspapers. Most of the woodwork in the house is original, but the McHenrys fell on hard times during the depression, and when an antiques dealer happened to visit the house during this period, he persuaded them to sell some of the beautifully carved mantels. They were replaced with plain wooden mantels salvaged from former servants' quarters. "They never fit as well," says Mrs. Hicky regretfully.

History is personal in the South, and in Southern houses every picture, as the truism has it, tells a story. A particularly powerful image is a portrait in the parlor showing John McHenry (Dan's grandfather) as a boy at school at the Georgia Military Institute, wearing the uniform in which he and his class offered themselves for duty in the Confederate army in 1864. He was then fifteen years old.

When houses were built in the early 1800s, taxes were imposed on every room, and since a closet was considered a room, few built-in closets existed. Instead, huge armoires had to be carried up to the bedrooms. (The built-in closets in the bedrooms of the Stokes-McHenry house were added between

ABOVE: *The handsome, brass early-nineteenth-century front-door knocker is engraved with the name McHenry.* ABOVE LEFT: *In the parlor, a lamp bears the name of Zoe, a light to the legend of a woman who literally stopped traffic with her beauty. It operates by touch.* OPPOSITE RIGHT: *On the Hickys's fifty-second wedding anniversary, their son Stratton gave them a Barbie doll collector's set of Scarlett O'Hara and Rhett Butler. A crystal horn of plenty symbolizes their long marriage.* OPPOSITE LEFT: *One of the family treasures is this passport, dated 1859, belonging to John McHenry, allowing him to travel, "accompanied by his wife."*

1849 and 1852.) Every house, however, had one built-in closet that was tax-exempt—the crawl space under the main stairs. This invaluable storage space, often stretching back into the darkness, was always stuffed with family items, saved and forgotten for generations. The Stokes-McHenry house is no exception. Open the door under the stairs and one sees, in telling juxtaposition the rusting metal frames of a set of hoop skirts (including children's) and, resting beside them, an old shotgun.

As for the staircase itself, it is the object of one of those Civil War anecdotes every self-respecting Southern family volunteers at the slightest opportunity. During the fighting, a family member was shot in downtown Madison, and he struggled, bleeding and increasingly weak, to his daughter's home, with Union soldiers in hot pursuit. The housekeeper at the house begged them to allow the wounded man to die in peace, and he later died on the stairs from loss of blood. "Right *there*," Dan says, pointing dramatically to the spot. "As a child I refused to put my foot on that step." His wife beams at her husband's memory. "It's fun to go back and talk about the past," she says.

Perhaps the most poignant image of family life in this intensely personal house is the children's playroom on the second floor. It is filled with toys going back five generations. When Hattie-Mina Hicky enters this diminutive wonderland, she affectionately rearranges the dolls and caresses the miniature furniture. "Look at this stove," she marvels. "I think it still works." She smiles with a distant expression in her eyes, as though sensing in that room the pleasure of all the generations of children who have played there before.

The hall is wide, in proportion with the front door (which was known as a "coffin door," being wide enough for a coffin to pass through). The Chippendale-style, glass-fronted secretary is filled with letters dating back to the 1800s. A bust of Shakespeare stands approvingly on a shelf amidst a set of Harvard Classics.

DINGLEWOOD
COLUMBUS, GEORGIA

The long central hallway can accommodate oversized furniture,
such as the Bowers's plantation desk (in the background) and the three-seater sofa
upholstered in yellow damask. The extremely ornate ceiling ornamentation
reflects the imposing architecture of the house.

Columbus, at the western edge
of Georgia, is a small town that expanded
rapidly along the banks of the Chattahoochee
River in the early 1800s, when plantation fortunes
were being made. Transportation of cotton and
tobacco depended on easy river access, and
Columbus benefited from its position on this big
waterway. The town is famous for its neighbor,
Fort Benning, as well as for its role in the Civil War
as a munitions center. Several fine plantation
houses still exist in Columbus, one of the most
interesting being Dinglewood, owned by the
late Lloyd G. Bowers and his wife, Effie,
who lives here still.

The generous wraparound piazza with columns and
floor-length dark green shutters, punctuated by statuary, emphasizes
the dignity of this 1850s plantation house.

Started in the mid-1850s, Dinglewood was built later than most of the classic antebellum mansions, reaching completion only two or so years before the outbreak of the Civil War. This late entry explains much of its lavishness. By the late 1850s annual exports of Georgia cotton neared seven hundred thousand bales, and Dinglewood's architecture reflects the huge profits reaped from those exports. Like the great Fifth Avenue mansions of the robber barons toward the end of the nineteenth-century, Dinglewood makes a grand statement, glorifying that moment in Southern history when plantation owners had reached a pinnacle of financial and social success. The moment was brief, but Dinglewood, almost more than any other house in the Deep South, still reflects that starry conjunction of taste, sophistication, and wealth that these people so fleetingly enjoyed.

The house was built by Colonel Early Hurt for his daughter, Julia. Colonel Hurt was rich and successful and nothing was too good for his beloved daughter. He gave her a two-story Italianate villa, with columns, a stucco facade, and a cupola. The architects were a local Columbus partnership, Barringer and Morton. They were clearly responding to the current fashion in the 1850s for the Italian look that had been widely promoted by Philadelphia architect Samuel Sloan, and whose work in Montgomery and Natchez was extensively copied. Italian craftsmen were imported from Europe to Dinglewood to carve and install the interior's crown moldings and decorative fretwork. (They lived in cottages on the estate.) One can see from the decorative cornices that still remain how

ABOVE: *Most of the marble statuary in the house was brought back from Italy by the present owner's grandparents.* OPPOSITE: *The front door, with its transom, ornate pediment, and double Corinthian pillars, makes a formidable entrance.*

RIGHT: *The drawing room is dominated by a huge mirror, made in Italy specially for Dinglewood and the house's first owner, Colonel Early Hurt. The marble mantelpiece, like those in the rest of the house, was also imported at this time from Italy.* OPPOSITE: *The music room is like a twin to the drawing room, each flowing into the other via a wide opening with sliding doors. An identical mirror to that in the drawing room, also originating in Italy, hangs on the wall; the curtain treatments in both rooms are similar. The elaborate crown moldings are a contribution of imported Italian craftsmen.*

talented these artists were, and one can imagine how expensive they must have been.

Of course, Dinglewood was not the only house in Columbus furnished in this luxurious style. Colonel Hurt's friends had also become rich and increasingly knowledgeable about art and design. By the mid-1850s transportation up the Chattahoochee River from Europe and the northeastern coast of the United States had become much easier, and top-quality furniture, textiles, and artworks from Italy, France, England, New York, and Philadelphia were now a constant feature of the river traffic. Special inlets were created so that these valuable treasures could be delivered right to the plantation house doors.

Julia Hurt seems to have been worthy of her father's extravagance. She was by all accounts a beauty, and made a good marriage to Colonel Peyton Colquitt. After he was killed at

The dining room is filled with inherited furniture. The table comes from Philadelphia; the mahogany chairs and sideboards from Mrs. Bowers's Charleston family. The long, high windows are framed in an alcove, separated by a French pier mirror. The marble statues were brought back from Italy in the 1880s by Mrs. Bowers's grandparents.

the Battle of Chickamauga in 1863, however, Julia and her mother left Georgia and moved to France. There Julia met and had a romantic liaison with her late husband's West Point classmate Jerome Napoleon Bonaparte, Napoleon's nephew. So great was his feeling for her that he gave her an elegant gold brooch, which came back with her to Dinglewood when she returned home at the end of the Civil War. (Bonaparte later married an American and died in Baltimore, Maryland, in 1870.) Julia remarried but had no children, and after her death the house went to relatives. The brooch was inherited by her goddaughter Julia Bowers and later given to Lloyd and Effie Bowers, who keep it safe at Dinglewood.

The house was passed down through a succession of family members until 1940, when it was purchased by a speculator. After it had been left empty for two years, in 1948 Lloyd and Effie Bowers bought it, returning it to its family roots. (Lloyd's aunt was named after the romantic Julia, daughter of Dinglewood's first owner.)

It seems a miracle that so much of the original architecture remains. Of course, a lot of work had to be done on the house when the Bowers family moved in. There was no insulation, windows were broken, and electricity and plumbing were in disrepair. But in spite of its long neglect, no structural restoration was required. As for the interiors, again fortune

ABOVE LEFT: *A portrait of Effie Bowers's grandfather Rudolph Siegling in his Confederate uniform hangs over the dining room fireplace.*
ABOVE RIGHT: *A mahogany Chippendale secretary in the living room displays a collection of French and English china.*

ABOVE LEFT: One of the guest rooms is painted a bird's-egg blue and has mahogany tester beds and unmatched furniture from Charleston. The marble fireplace, made in Italy, is original.

LEFT: In many Southern families, when a mother or mother-in-law grows older she comes back to the family house where a room, most often the parlor as in this case, is made over into her bedroom. The mahogany bed and furniture come from Charleston. The mahogany door, like all the doors on the ground floor, is hung with silver hinges.

OPPOSITE: On the imposing stairwell and landing, niches were specially designed to showcase the beautiful sculptures imported from Italy, flooded with light from a Palladian-style window.

ABOVE: *The Italianate façade of Dinglewood is glimpsed at the end of a green curtain of huge old magnolia trees.* ABOVE RIGHT: *One can view the grounds from one end of the piazza.*

smiled. The ceiling and door moldings and elaborately carved Italian marble fireplaces still dominate the drawing room, parlor, and music room, vivid reminders of those Italian craftsmen first brought here by Colonel Early Hurt. The huge gilt mirrors enhance the impression of extravagance. Inherited furniture has been added, providing warmth and meaning to these formal spaces. For instance, in the hall is an old plantation desk, six feet long, where Lloyd Bowers's grandfather used to issue his directions that helped run the blockade during the Civil War, selling cotton overseas in exchange for guns.

Effie Bowers grew up in Charleston, and many of the fine pieces of furniture and artworks now at Dinglewood come from her cultivated Charleston family. "My grandparents collected art," she explains. "In the 1880s they made trips to Europe and brought back sculpture and paintings." There are other mementoes of her Charleston past—on the upstairs landing, for instance, there are framed copies of the *Courier*, the Charleston newspaper owned by her family after the Civil War. One is dated 1803; the other, with a black border, is dated April 26, 1865, the day Lincoln was shot.

Dinglewood's interior has survived remarkably intact over these turbulent years and its exterior still consists of the magnificent double-columned front door, wraparound piazza, peach stucco facade, and splendid Italianate cupola. Still, the house has suffered the fate of many of these great antebellum estates in decline over the decades, as their owners are forced by economic necessity to surrender what is left of their land. In 1920 two maiden ladies who inherited Dinglewood had the foresight to consult with a developer in order to collaborate on a plan that would offend as little as possible the original landscape. The result is a development of several large neo–manor houses constructed around a circular road, with Dinglewood as its crown.

In spite of diminished surroundings, the house retains its power. A row of huge magnolia trees forms a dramatic allée up the brick walkway that leads from the perimeter road to the beautiful front entrance of the mansion. The tall, dark, glossy-leaved trees separate the house from its neighbors, casting ancient shade and giving notice that history, when it is written in bricks and mortar, cannot be eradicated.

ABOVE LEFT: *The spacious piazza, so typical of Southern houses, is enhanced by the tall windows with unusually large sets of six glass panes and by the strategically placed statuary.*
ABOVE: *Floor-to-transom shutters conceal a side entry.*

SHIELDS-ETHRIDGE FARM

JEFFERSON, GEORGIA

The schoolhouse, founded by Ira Ethridge in 1909, still has three of the original desks, from which the rest are copied. The walls are made of beaded wood.

History is sometimes difficult to visualize, but the Shields-Ethridge Farm, situated in a rural, hilly landscape not far from Atlanta, offers even the most frugal imagination a banquet. The basic elements of a working plantation are all in place here, including a cotton gin, blacksmith's shop, grist mill, tenant house, commissary, a small schoolhouse, and two family cemeteries. As well as the physical evidence that surrounds the property, inside the plantation house there is a treasure trove of family documents dating back to the late 1700s, vividly depicting the life of Georgian planters over two hundred years. The Shields-Ethridge Farm is the real thing—not a tourist replica in aspic, not a scholarly reconstruction, but an authentic survivor of generations of struggle and accomplishment.

CLOCKWISE FROM TOP LEFT: *The blacksmith's shop still has its anvil and forge, as well as a fire pit, dated 4/12/1907, along with ploughs and logging carts. The commissary provided supplies for the farm and community, including butter (made by Susan Ella Shields-Ethridge), salt, soap, snuff, hardware, seeds, sacks, catalogs, plough parts, and mule gear. Cotton gins, now lined up in silence, were once hugely noisy machines turning white, fluffy balls into five-hundred–pound bales of cotton. In the commissary, the old advertisements, canisters of tea and varied dry goods, and Sears Roebuck catalogs are as evocative of the period as a film set—only they are authentic.*

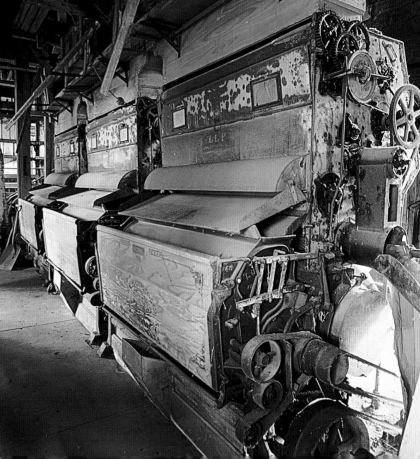

Joseph Shields came to Georgia from Virginia in 1796 and acquired the property through Indian land grants during the first white settlements around 1800. (In the family records are Jackson County tax receipts dating from 1802.) Shields worked 294 acres very profitably here and willed the land to his son James, who died in 1863, leaving his wife, Charity, like so many Southern war widows, to take over the responsibility of running the farm. She did a splendid job, continuing to produce wheat, corn, oats, and cotton until 1866, when her two sons, William and Joseph Robert, returned home from fighting

The dining room of the Shields-Ethridge house has nineteenth-century furniture and furnishings. The still life of fruit has "been here for eons," says Mrs. Ethridge.

with the Confederate army in Virginia. (After the Shields family freed their slaves in 1865, at least some of them asked to stay on the farm. In the family archive there is a copy of agreement between Charity Shields and several former slaves dated that same year.)

Joseph Robert's daughter, Susan Ella, married Ira Washington Ethridge in 1896 and then moved to the farm to care for her father. At his death in 1908 she inherited the thriving property. Ira Ethridge turned out to be as significant a figure as the family into which he had married—"a big man," as his granddaughter, Susan Ethridge Chaisson, describes him—and he extended the scope of the plantation with vision. The family, now in its eighth generation, lives here still.

The main plantation house was built by Joseph Robert Shields in 1866, shortly after returning from the war. In contrast to some of the grand antebellum mansions in Louisiana and lower Mississippi, it is a sturdy, no-nonsense building, showing the practical character of its owner and the austere mood of the times. The roof of the house was originally shin-

gled and had a federal-style wood-latticed porch. In 1914 Ira Ethridge removed the porch and added four Greek-Revival-style columns, giving the house more dignity and stature. (The date is marked on a step in front of the house; Ira Ethridge was proud of his work and always dated his contributions.)

Ira Ethridge made many other important changes to the property. In the early 1900s he installed a cotton gin (Eli Whitney's steam-generated machine that separated the seed from the cotton and revolutionized production). He also added a threshing machine and grist mill, as well as extending the acreage of the property. In 1909, having ascertained by census that there were twenty-six white children living in the community, he was granted state money to help build a school. A house for the black teacher, known as the teacher's house, not far from the main farmhouse, was constructed in 1915.

This almost feudal system was carefully managed by the lord of the manor. Ira Ethridge's patronage extended not only to farming and education but also to commerce. He opened a commissary to provide supplies for the farm and community.

The large breakfront in the parlor has been passed down through the family. In it are books, dolls, angels, carved animals, and old cameras, such as an antique Kodak that "still takes the most excellent pictures," declares Mrs. Ethridge. The wooden horse dates from the 1880s. The light fixture is 1900s.

The shop sold everything from farm equipment to sacks of grain, from fresh vegetables to formula for killing the boll weevil (a sinister mixture of molasses, saccharine, ice cream, and calcium arsonate, which was spread over the fields with a mop). The commissary also sold butter, made by Susan Ella, with her stamp ELLA on each block.

Ira and Susan Ella Ethridge had only one child, Ira Lanis, who, on the death of his parents, inherited the plantation. He phased out cotton ginning in the late 1950s. "The land was really too hilly for successful cotton growing, unlike the flat lands in South Georgia," Susan Chaisson explains. Moreover, the boll weevil, in spite of the molasses concoction, continued to devastate crops. "Also," she adds, "we needed updated equipment and it was very expensive." So Lanis focused on cattle and grain, which are still the mainstays of the farm. Lanis married Joyce Storey in 1944, producing two daughters, Susan and Ann. After his death in 1970 Joyce, like her female forebears, assumed the running of the plantation.

True to form, her daughter Susan, with her husband, Darrell, and their three children, Darrell Jr., Betsy, and Bobby, has moved into the house to help her mother, while Joyce's other daughter, Ann, and husband, Bob Lacey, with their two sons, Bobby and Taylor, live in Valdosta, Georgia, returning to help on special farm days and provide modern technological skills, such as manning the farm's website. The eighth generation of the family has just got its start—Ethridge Paul Chaisson, firstborn son of Darrell Jr. and his wife, Shane.

Thus the pattern repeats itself. The sense of continuity is

LEFT: *An Empire curved-glass cabinet in the dining room contains family silver and china, and a collection of Depression glass that is in everyday use.*
BELOW: *A photograph of Joyce Beatrice Storey Ethridge, aged twelve, sits on a shelf in the parlor breakfront, along with books, old cameras, and other mementoes.*

ABOVE: *The old cemetery, nestling in the woods, dates from 1834. The stone markers are carved with names of the family dead.* OPPOSITE: *The commissary was built around 1909 and its wooden siding and tin roof still stand, protecting the fascinating and historic treasures within.*

overwhelming. Since the early 1800s the same family has owned and farmed the land, each generation adding to the property according to the economics and culture of the time, producing not a time warp, but a constant cycle of reseeding, each time growing into new green shoots of family history. The cotton gin still stands ready to receive the white, fluffy puffballs that made so many planters so immensely wealthy. The blacksmith's shop still has the anvil and forge where the iron was fired. Perhaps the most evocative of all the surviving buildings is the commissary, which was not cleaned out until the early 1990s. Under the decades of dust and junk, the family found, still set out on the counters, many of the original stocks of goods that were sold to customers all those years ago. There was even a string of dried onions hanging from the rafters.

Recently, Susan Ethridge Chaisson and her mother, Joyce, came upon a small box in the attic, inside which was a wad of documents tightly packed in rag paper that had not been opened for maybe a century. Carefully unwrapping the paper, she and her mother marveled at the materials it revealed, many dating back to the 1700s—purchase orders, agreements, tax records, the working records of a busy family.

"Finding things like this that date back to well before the Civil War, we feel responsible for taking care of them and preserving them for the next generation," Susan says, sighing at the daunting thought. "For instance," her mother adds, "we even found the receipt for a lead bathtub that had been shipped to my father-in-law nearly one hundred years ago. I always wondered how on earth it got here."

CARNEGIE ESTATE

CUMBERLAND ISLAND, GEORGIA

*Although Carnegie Estate's Plum Orchard is no longer inhabited, there
are still signs of George Carnegie's elegant life in this glimpse of an enfilade of rooms—
walnut paneling, oak furniture, a Tiffany lamp, and a now-silent grand piano.*

Cumberland Island is a remote
subtropical barrier island off the Atlantic coast,
reachable only by ferry from Fernandina Beach or by
private boat or plane. It is eighteen miles long, the
largest barrier island in Georgia, with seven hundred
acres of freshwater wetlands and more untouched
beach than anywhere on the eastern seaboard. This
astonishing diversity of natural environments creates a
treasure trove of wildlife, from feral hogs, armadillos,
pelicans, loggerhead turtles, egrets, herons, and
seabirds of every kind to herds of wonderful wild
horses, which were brought to the island by the
Spaniards in the fifteenth century and, after
generations of inbreeding, were strengthened by
Appaloosa herds imported from the American West.

*A large, upholstered Empire sofa decorates the
upstairs landing of Greyfield; over it, a portrait of the Carnegie family.*

ABOVE: *Old cars, loved but abandoned, are lined up in a dignified row on the grounds of Dungeness, the original Carnegie mansion, now itself a ruin.* OPPOSITE: *Plum Orchard is the most imposing house on the Carnegie Estate. Consisting of 117 rooms, the central part, with Greek Revival portico and pediment, was built in 1898 and the two large wings were added in 1903.*

The island was originally inhabited by Timucua Indians. In the 1500s the Spaniards occupied it. After they departed, Revolutionary War general Nathanael Greene bought it and built a house here called Dungeness. The house was destroyed by fire a hundred years later, and the island was once again largely abandoned, except for a plantation owner named Robert Stafford, who grew sea island cotton, rice, and indigo there. In 1881 Thomas Carnegie, younger brother of the more famous Andrew Carnegie, partners in Carnegie Brothers Steel, came here with his wife, Lucy, acquiring land from Stafford to build a house as a vacation retreat. Thomas died at the age of forty-two of pneumonia, leaving Lucy with nine children to raise here.

Ninety percent of the island is now owned by the National Park Service. The other 10 percent is owned by the Ferguson family, Thomas Carnegie's direct descendants. Their estate, headed by Janet ("Gogo") Carnegie Ferguson and her husband, David Sayre, now numbers about thirty people, the total permanent population of the island. This disposition of land between private citizens and a public institution is unprecedented and almost came to grief some years ago when government officials attempted to wrest ownership of the remaining land from the family. Thanks to the uncompromising negotiations of Margaret Ferguson, Gogo's mother, the family managed to retain their island property in perpetuity.

Thomas and Lucy Carnegie began building their first house on the site of General Greene's vanished home, naming it Dungeness in the general's honor, but sadly Thomas died

RIGHT: *A portrait of Gogo's grandmother adds a dashing touch to the living room of Greyfield. On the table are a sea turtle skull and a huge bronze dinner gong now used as a container. The curtains date from the 1960s.* OPPOSITE: *A sense of family permeates the interior of the house Gogo and her family built in 1992. On a table under a portrait of Gogo by West Frazier are family photographs, including one of Gogo's grandmother Lucy. A collection of baskets hangs nearby.*

before his great mansion was finished. Lucy immediately took up the reins and later set about building more houses on the island as wedding presents for her large brood. Her son George received the grandest one. It was called Plum Orchard, and it was designed in the most imposing Greek Revival style, with four Ionic columns, an elegantly decorated pediment, arched windows, and balustrades. The central part of the house went up in 1898, and two large wings were added later. The house has 117 rooms, a billiard room, and an indoor pool, a very unusual feature for its time. Furnished with Tiffany lamps, dark walnut paneling, and oak furniture, it was testament to the Carnegies' position at that time. Now unlived in and neglected, it has become a worrisome burden for its current owner, the National Park Service. Another children's house, Stafford Place, burned down in 1901. (Fire has always been a threat on this heavily forested island.) Lucy Carnegie died in 1916, after which Dungeness was abandoned. As though doomed by fate like its forebear, the house burned down in 1959. Its ruined walls, along with stables and outbuildings, still remain as reminders of its former glory.

Stafford Links Golf Cup
Presented by a humble member
UNCLE ANDREW
New York April 12th
1899
Won by
W. C. CARNEGIE

IT IS VERY BAD
TO PUT ANYTHING
AWAY UNWASHED
IE: FLOWER THINGS
LEFT WITH WATER ....
DON'T DO IT
CLEAN
CLEAN

U.S. MAIL   U.S.   U.S.

Rachel Garrett   Fred_?   Schooners

SKIP   Caroline & Jill   Karma   Daniel   Sprague

Fawn   Hadley   MIKER   AMIE

ABOVE: *The living room of Greyfield has a typical Southern feel; at the far end, a wall of books belonging to Lucy Carnegie, many with her bookplate in the flyleaf.* OPPOSITE, CLOCKWISE FROM TOP LEFT: *In the library corner of the living room, a circular table holds books, toys, and a large globe that, according to Gogo, has "been here always." A silver golf trophy is one of the many mementoes of the Carnegie family. Inside Greyfield, this small collection of mail boxes belongs to the island residents, all of whom come here to pick up their mail. The silver closet is crammed with old family silver, not much used these days, as is clear by the instructions to "clean" on various items.*

LEFT: *The bleached beams in the ceiling come from recycled docks and other lumber found on the island.* OPPOSITE: *The guest bedroom has a tropical feel with pale walls, simple mahogany furniture, and a Caribbean bamboo bed.*

The most important of the Carnegie houses still standing is Greyfield, built in 1901 for Lucy Carnegie's daughter, Margaret. It is a classic Southern plantation house, practical and elegant at the same time. Raised up from its foundations to let breezes through and to prevent damp, it has an enclosed second-story verandah built over a porch that stretches the full length of the front facade. In the rear of the house, a small Greek Revival-style portico and balustrade face outward to the live oaks with their heavy swags of moss that offer shade not only in the garden but throughout the two-hundred-acre property as well.

Greyfield is now an inn, but it still has the feel of a private house, with all the Carnegie furniture and furnishings in place. The family spirit retains its power in these largely untouched turn-of-the century rooms. Guests may wander among Lucy Carnegie's books and wedding presents, look into memento-stuffed cabinets, drink their coffee surrounded by portraits and family treasures. One glass-fronted cabinet is filled with toys, scrimshaw, games, and even a miniature frog orchestra. But do not attempt to reach inside to touch these objects. "Oh, we lost the key some time ago," explains a family member, waving vaguely at it. "That cabinet hasn't been opened for fifty years."

In 1992 Gogo and David, following family tradition, built themselves another house, called Godahalu (after the first letters of the names Gogo, David, Hannah, their daughter, and Lucy, the matriarch). A deceptively modest bungalow on the outside, inside is a series of light, airy rooms, including a spacious living room with a high ceiling supported by beams rescued from docks and lumber found on the island. The house is filled with family heirlooms, photographs, and mementoes.

Gogo's brother Mitty lives in another house on the estate. He is home-schooling his daughter, Hadley, so she does not have to leave Cumberland Island even for her education. Hadley's teacher goes over on the ferry from the mainland to take up her daily duties, and on one occasion she remarked to a visitor how much her eleven-year-old pupil loved the island. "She has a reverence for the place," her instructor said. *Reverence* is a strong word to use to describe a child's feeling for her home, but Cumberland Island is considered almost sacred in the eyes of the dynasty that has inhabited it for so long, and the wild beauty of this place that has been in the family for more than one hundred years continues to work its magic on each succeeding generation.

OPPOSITE TOP LEFT: *The hallway has an interior arch, a hundred-year-old case clock, and a Chinese lacquer cabinet. The portrait is of Lucy Carnegie's father.* OPPOSITE TOP RIGHT: *An antique clock sits in front of a photograph of Margaret Carnegie in her wedding dress.* BOTTOM: *The wainscot-lined attic as a montage of family history: riding boots, old golf clubs, steamer trunks, discarded shoes, and photographs. Nothing gets thrown away.*

FLORIDA

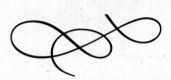

There was something in the very atmosphere of a small town in the Deep South, something spooked-up and romantic, which did extravagant things to the imagination... It had something to do with long and heavy afternoons with nothing doing.

WILLIE MORRIS, "NORTH TOWARD HOME"

STOCKTON-CURRY HOUSE
QUINCY, FLORIDA

This was Elizabeth Dickson's grandfather's bedroom.
A family wedding dress hangs on the door. On the mantel are
pictures of Greg Dickson's parents, who came from Scotland.

Florida may not be considered as Southern
a state as Georgia or Louisiana. It was a late bloomer
in relation to its sister states, gaining admission to
statehood only in 1845 after wars between Seminole
Indians and American settlers had been concluded. At
this time, southern Florida was untamed wilderness,
and the state's main political and economic centers
were St. Augustine and Pensacola. By the middle of
the nineteenth century, however, middle Florida, as
the northwestern region stretching along the Gulf of
Mexico was called, had become by far the most
prosperous section of the state, with huge cotton and
tobacco plantations manned by over half of the
approximately sixty-one thousand slaves living and
working in Florida. With Tallahassee, strategically
positioned halfway between St. Augustine and
Pensacola, having been designated the state capital, the
wealthy plantation owners in middle Florida carried
enormous political influence in the state.

The Stockton-Curry house was built in 1842 in one of the most popular architectural styles of the period—Greek Revival—with four fluted columns, a large pediment above a two-story portico, and shutters.

ABOVE: *A wrought-iron garden chair and table are placed in a shady part of the richly planted garden.* OPPOSITE: *A few yards from the Stockton-Curry house is a charming smaller version, also with columns and a pediment, built in approximately 1872 as a law office for the then-house-owner, Philip Stockton, Jr.*

Quincy was founded in 1825. Situated at the heart of Gadsden County twenty miles west of Tallahassee, it was geographically well placed in the center of this booming region and benefited from the area's prosperity, quickly becoming a flourishing agricultural town with thriving education and religious institutions and busy river traffic. Quincy became a classic Southern town, with many plantation houses and a downtown area now designated as a National Register Historic District. During the Civil War no decisive battles were fought on Florida soil, and Union soldiers never penetrated the interior of the state, thus Quincy's old mansions have remained relatively intact.

In 1842 the continuing economic expansion of middle Florida brought Philip A. Stockton and his brother, William, scions of a successful New Jersey and Pennsylvania family, to the region. The Stocktons' plan was to set up and operate a line of mail coaches between St. Augustine and Mobile, Alabama. They settled first in Marianna, Florida, but moved in 1843 to Quincy, where Philip Stockton bought a fine new townhouse from Isaac R. Harris, who had built it only a year earlier. The two-story wooden house, very little changed since Stockton's time, is in typical antebellum style. It has a Greek Revival facade with four fluted columns and a pediment decorated with a circular cartouche. Beneath the portico on the second floor, French doors open on to a small balustraded veranda. The interior is symmetrically proportioned, with square rooms and long, high sash windows. The central hallway is unusually large, allowing cool air to circulate in the

ABOVE: *An Empire dresser in the hall holds unsorted family photographs.*
OPPOSITE: *In the large, airy, white-painted hall, a portrait of Elizabeth Dickson's great-grandmother Mary Jane Shaw is over the dresser.*

ABOVE: *In a bedroom, the wallpaper dates from Elizabeth Dickson's grandmother's time. The portrait is of her grandmother Elizabeth Sloan Monroe Curry.* OPPOSITE: *In the upstairs hall, books and other antiques serve as a backdrop to a selection of nightgowns belonging to adults and children dating from the early 1900s. The portraits are of the Currys' great-grandparents.*

summertime, and eight of the rooms have fireplaces to provide heat on colder days.

It is not recorded whether the Stocktons ever pulled off their mail coach project, but both brothers survived the Civil War. It is not known how Philip served, but William became a colonel in the Confederate army, and after being captured at the Battle of Missionary Ridge, the Tennessee site of an important Union victory on November 25, 1863, he was imprisoned on an island in Lake Erie.

In the 1870s Philip Stockton Jr. built a separate law office a few feet from the main house, in the same Greek Revival style. Stockton died at home and passed on the house to his daughter, Martha Broome, who was the daughter-in-law of James E. Broome, governor of Florida from 1853 to 1857. In 1902 the Curry family bought the house, and their descendants live there still.

The Currys had been well established in Quincy by this time. Horace Curry was a partner in the Florida Tobacco Company, on East Franklin Street, handling the largest volume of tobacco business in the state during the first ten years of the

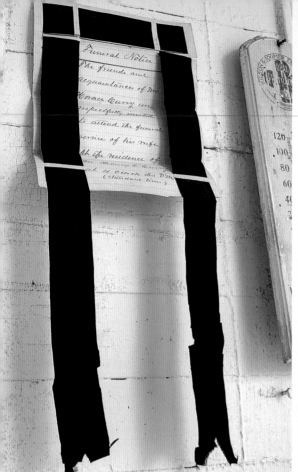

ABOVE: The funeral notice, edged in black grosgrain ribbon, of Horace Curry's wife, dating from the early 1890s, inviting friends to attend the funeral service "at the residence of Mr. Henry C. Curry at 4 o'clock pm (standard time)." ABOVE RIGHT: A rare treasure— Elizabeth's grandmother's wedding book bound in a white silk cover, dated June 16, 1925, with ribbons, party favors, cake holders, and flower decorations saved from the event. RIGHT: In the attic, a wicker laundry basket and boxes of old clothes, hats, and shoes keep the past alive.

twentieth century. Other members of the Curry family were local businessmen, playing important roles in the running of the town. Elizabeth Curry Dickson, Horace Curry's great-granddaughter, reckons, "We're related to everyone in Quincy."

The house reflects that strong sense of family. Every room has objects, portraits of ancestors, and shelves of mementoes that return the Curry family to its roots. There are old wedding dresses; Elizabeth Curry's grandmother's wedding book dated 1925; the death notice of the first wife of Horace Curry in the early 1890s; family trees; old shotguns and cavalry sabers found in the attic. The name Elizabeth seems to go back several generations. "We are all named after our grandparents," Elizabeth Dickson explains. "The same names are everywhere."

Dr. Calvin Curry, Elizabeth's father and the owner of the house, is currently renovating it, with the help of Elizabeth and her husband, Greg. They have stripped the interior flooring, revealing hand-sawn longleaf pine throughout the house. Now in its cleaned-up state, it has the striking appearance of cherry wood. The Dicksons are repainting the walls, which had been very dark, to the subtle shades of the period and returning the wood moldings, which had been painted black, to their proper color. "We took off a banister and found the original stain," explains Greg Dickson. Restoring an old building is always controversial, but the Dicksons have enormous respect for the architectural past of their home. Their hard work and attention to detail will allow the Stockton-Curry House, instead of the prospect of demolition, a return to health, and its survival will provide future generations with the stable embrace of family history.

ALABAMA

Only Miss Emily's house was left,
lifting its stubborn and coquettish decay above the
cotton wagons and the gasoline pumps.

—WILLIAM FAULKNER, "A ROSE FOR EMILY"

WINTER PLACE

MONTGOMERY, ALABAMA

*In the foreground, the North House of Winter Place stands dark,
now uninhabited. Behind it, joined by a passageway, is the Italianate South House,
where Winter Thorington still lives.*

Few cities express the clashing wills, desires, and dreams of the South as violently as Montgomery, Alabama. History confronts history in this battle-scarred city, its name branded forever on the American conscience. The center of Montgomery, once considered one of the most beautiful cities in the South, encapsulates its polarized past. A long, wide avenue leads up to the imposing neoclassical state capitol at the far end. On the steps of this building in 1861, Jefferson Davis was inaugurated as first president of the Confederacy. A little way down from this monument to the Old South is a modest redbrick church whose symbolism is just as significant as that of its grand neighbor. For here, a century later, in the Dexter Avenue King Memorial Baptist Church, Martin Luther King Jr. inspired his followers with a call to freedom from the tyranny of racial segregation. From Civil War to civil rights within a city block—the conjunction is breathtaking. The story of Winter Place, a strange, hallucinatory estate not far from these evocative sites, seems somehow to reflect the conflicting currents that for so long swirled around this city.

In the South House, antique furniture and a faded damask wallcovering recall the glamorous past.

ABOVE: *The interior staircase to the second floor of the South House is very narrow. The door moldings and banisters are still intact and show their quality.* OPPOSITE: *A fine mantel and twin doors still give dignity to this otherwise abandoned room, with a family portrait of Admiral Raphael Semmes, commander of the Confederate cruiser CSS Alabama, gazing across the empty floor.*

By the middle of the 1800s Montgomery had become the center of Alabama's hugely successful cotton industry. Its success translated into power, and it was designated the state capital in 1846. During these years, huge townhouses were built, testament to the great fortunes being made from the two C's, commerce and cotton. One of the finest was a dashing Italianate villa built around 1851 by the famous Philadelphia architect Samuel Sloan, for Colonel Joseph Samuel Prince Winter and his wife, Mary. But three years later, Winter's extensive business empire collapsed, and the family had to abandon Sloan's masterpiece. After several moves, in 1858 they began to build two houses on a triangular block of what is now South Goldthwaite Street. The timing was not good. The Civil War interrupted their progress, and as the Union raiders grew nearer with their promise to devastate Montgomery, the Winter family left Alabama for New York.

Joseph Winter returned to Montgomery in 1871 and finally finished the two houses. Called Winter Place, the North House was designed in a restrained Italianate style with little ornamentation; the South House, on the other hand, suggesting Joseph Winter's nostalgia for his original Sloan-designed mansion, has a cupola, a mansard roof, and elegant balustrades. It is surrounded by a dry moat, perhaps to collect water that would otherwise threaten the foundations. The houses are joined by an enclosed passageway, and it is said that at one time the entire family, including Joseph's three children and eleven grandchildren, lived in these two houses.

During the first decades of the twentieth century, Winter

ABOVE: *Light streams in through the threadbare curtain of a window that once looked out on to starry nights of music and parties.* OPPOSITE: *Icons of the Old South remain forever young in Winter Thorington's bedroom.*

Place was one of the social hubs of Montgomery, and people remember elegant lawn parties and dances and musical evenings there. But the Winters again fell on hard times. The North House was sold and for a while was used as a brothel during World War II. The South House, however, remained in the Winters' possession, and is now lived in by a member of the last generation of the family, Winter Thorington, Joseph's one and only great-great-grandson.

For a while it looked as though Thorington, the last of Joseph's line, would recapture some of the family glory. Handsome and charming, he enjoyed an aristocratic education at Exeter and Harvard and, after serving in the war, returned to Montgomery, buying back the North House and taking up permanent residence in Winter Place. He threw parties, acquired notoriety, and was a friend of all the interesting people in town, including Zelda Fitzgerald.

However, Winter Thorington, like some of his forebears, seemed destined to forfeit the benefits of worldly success. Never married, he is seventy-seven years old now, and much has changed at Winter Place. He lives in the South House, upstairs on the first floor, alone—on occasion without telephone or heat. The building is forsaken, almost derelict. Its once proud twin, the North House, is completely abandoned, and the passageway between them is crumbling, impassable. As shutters bang and tree limbs groan in the wind, visitors pick their way through the overgrown garden wondering if they are imagining, mingled with the sounds of neglect, the faint strains of an old swing band.

The gravestone reads:

SMOKEY
BELOVED CAT OF
WINTER & ORVILLE
BORN FRESNO, CALIF.
NOV. 1954
DIED MONTG, ALA.
FEB. 1962
TO LIVE IN HEARTS
WE LEFT BEHIND
IS NOT TO DIE

ABOVE: *In the garden, the grave of Winter Thorington's cat is sadly in need of restoration.* OPPOSITE TOP: *A yellow chair waits for Winter Thorington at the top of the stairs to the South House. The elegantly arched front door, with fine raised paneling, was a welcoming entryway for visitors.* OPPOSITE BOTTOM: *The passageway that joins the two houses, once humming with activity, now musters only ghosts.*

RIGHT: *While a red silk wallcovering shows its wear, Queen Victoria and Prince Albert survey an Empire-style marble-topped chest of drawers.* BELOW LEFT: *Original plans of the house and family photographs prove that Winter Place has known many years of good times.* BELOW RIGHT: *Nearly two hundred years of history cluster together on this dusty tabletop.* OPPOSITE: *A bedroom now has only mattress springs leaning against a Chippendale-style armoire, with an old bicycle propped up against it.*

ABOVE: *The heart pine wood paneling in the parlor (a wood that when polished, acquires a reddish cherry hue) still retains its beauty. Light flows in from a deeply recessed Italianate arched window. A portrait of Winter Thorington's grandmother Sallie hangs over the mantel.* OPPOSITE: *Southern history is the essence of countless biographies, and there is dignity in all of them.*

Winter Thorington is a familiar figure in the streets of Montgomery, greeting neighbors and stopping for an early morning breakfast at the farmers' market. People who remember the old days are concerned about Winter Place and wonder what can be done to help him save it. There is a move afoot to have it listed on the National Register of Historic Places, but even with this honorific title, hope is hard to come by for this once lively estate. As time completes its usual ruthless work, Winter Place's vibrant history seems to be playing out as little more than just another ghost story from that distant Southern world that is gone forever.

APPENDIX 1: DISTINCTIVE ARCHITECTURAL STYLES OF THE ANTEBELLUM SOUTH

THE GOLDEN AGE of Southern architecture took place between 1800 and 1860, when the plantation owners began to make their fortunes from cotton and tobacco and embarked on house-building projects to reflect their rapidly rising wealth and social status. A few architectural styles became the norm, owing to fashion, convenience, and the consciousness of man's position not only in the South but also in the world.

GEORGIAN

THE EARLY COLONISTS from England to America were often junior members of aristocratic families, and they brought with them the prevailing taste in houses, gardens, and furniture. In eighteenth-century England, the Georgian style was hugely popular—classical in form, with strictly proportioned walls, windows, and doors. These formally planned country estates became the accepted architectural form throughout England and were then transported to America, most notably to the state of Virginia. Berkeley, one of the James River Plantations, dating from 1726, is a fine example. The style was only occasionally exploited during the high days of the Old South, as preference for Greek Revival forms took precedence. Hints of the more full-blown Greek Revival can often be seen in early Georgian houses throughout the South, which were often made of brick, with pilasters, pedimented dormers, fluted columns, and double-hung sash windows.

GREEK REVIVAL

GREEK REVIVAL WAS BY FAR the most popular architectural style in the antebellum South. In the search for good taste and a sense of permanence, architects and their clients found their answer in the values of the ancient Greeks. The war of Greek independence against Turkey in 1812 inspired a new nationalism among Americans, who looked to ancient Greece for their models of democracy. The classical orders, marked by the distinctive decoration of Doric, Ionian, and Corinthian capitals, represented the noble principles of reason, beauty, and longevity that had been developed in the ancient world. (Roman domestic architecture also found a place at this time. Thomas Jefferson chose the work of Andrea Palladio as the model for his house, Monticello, in Virginia. Completed in 1809, it became a benchmark for aspiring neoclassicists.)

The Southern Greek Revival house typically follows a pattern consisting of a series of columns, porticos with ornamented pediments, architraves, and bracketed cornices. These architectural forms were largely copied from the classic Greek or Roman temple. The style became so popular that it was called Greek fever.

ITALIANATE

FOR THOSE UNHAPPY with the strict forms of Georgian and Greek revival architecture, a more fanciful, asymmetrical style became a popular alternative. Dubbed Italianate, its relation to Italian villas of the late Renaissance can be identified in the

typical combination of tall tower and two-story floor plan. Arched windows are inserted into loggias or arcades, the flat roof has widely projecting eaves, and the facade is finished generally with a softly tinted stucco. Tuscan country houses show similar layouts, with belvederes, verandas, and loggias, all thoroughly well suited to the Southern climate. The most familiar identifying feature of most of these houses is a decorative cupola on the roof. This elegant style found favor in rural settings in the South, encouraged by Italian landscape painting and the idea of the picturesque.

OCTAGONAL

THE IDEA OF AN octagonal house was particularly appealing to Southerners, who were always on the lookout for ways to keep their houses cool. The octagonal shape allows for breezes to form cross-drafts as they waft through the rooms. Although not many were actually built, since the form demanded special skills from builders, masons, and carpenters, there are some fine examples. The most famous octagonal house in the South is Longwood, in Natchez, designed by architect Samuel Sloan, for Dr. Halley Nutt. Longwood was begun in 1859, but when the Civil War broke out the project was halted. Dr. Nutt, a Union sympathizer, lost all his money and died at the age of forty-eight, leaving a wife and eight children in the half-built house. After the war the family abandoned it, and to this day the house has never been completed.

APPENDIX 2: DEFINING THE DECORATIVE ARTS OF THE OLD SOUTH

The interiors of the great ANTEBELLUM houses have many similarities, largely because they were all formed at roughly the same time—between 1820 and 1860. After that, time—and decorating—stopped. No new things were purchased; no old things were thrown out. What remains is a record of a particular time and taste, as expressed by the influential artists and craftsmen who were selected to furnish these halls, parlors, dining rooms, and bedrooms. Many names and decorative styles are the same, featured in house after house, acquired from the same sources, admired to the same degree. Although originating from very different backgrounds, assembled together they offer a strikingly unified vision of what, at the time, people in the South wanted to live with in their homes.

FURNITURE STYLES

Chippendale

THOMAS CHIPPENDALE (1718–1779) is the most famous cabinet-maker England ever produced. He worked mainly in the Rococo and neo-Gothic style. The delicacy and elegance of his designs, mostly carved in mahogany, immediately became the most popular choice for furnishing eighteenth-century interiors. His son continued the tradition, adding neoclassical motifs

to the designs, and by the mid-nineteenth century the Chippendale look had been copied everywhere and transported throughout Europe and America.

Empire

THE EMPIRE STYLE WAS developed in France at the turn of the nineteenth century, "Empire" referring to the empire of Napoleon (1804–1815). The furniture is distinguished by its heavy, solid appearance, often made in mahogany or other hardwoods, with decoration promoting imperial themes such as laurel wreaths and eagles. Pieces like armoires, four-poster beds, and sideboards lent themselves to the massiveness of the style. The Empire period also saw the rise in popularity of heavy curtains with sweeping valances and tentlike draperies, made of rich fabrics like velvet and damask, again reflecting the eminence of the imperial Frenchman, and satisfying Southern plantation owners' desire for a noble image.

Victorian

VICTORIAN FURNITURE IS closely related to that of the Empire style, but the Victorian influence was established somewhat later, Queen Victoria's dates ranging from 1837 to 1901. The Victorian style, like the Empire style, was heavy and ornate, often making use of industrial materials such as glass and brass. Victorian interiors are now regarded with some suspicion, so often appearing fussy and overstuffed and lacking design merit. For Southern interiors, however, where darkness, offering a respite from the bright sun, was often a blessing, the Victorian style, with its decorative confidence and sweeping shade, was greatly admired and copied.

Rococo Revival

ROCOCO REVIVAL STYLE BECAME very popular in the mid-nineteenth century. A reaction against the massiveness and hauteur of Empire furniture, the Rococo Revival referred back to the lighter, more highly ornamented style that followed the baroque period in the eighteenth century, although in the antebellum South it frequently appears as heavy and solid as its main stylistic competitors. The most famous proponent of the Rococo Revival style was German cabinetmaker John Henry Belter (1804–1863), who immigrated to America in 1844. His distinctive parlor sets—matching sofas and chairs in laminated rosewood, with floridly carved decoration and heavily tufted upholstery—were widely copied, and dominate many Southern interiors of the period.

ARCHITECTS AND ARTISTS

John James Audubon

JOHN JAMES AUDUBON was born in Haiti in 1785. His family moved to France just before the French Revolution, at which point young Audubon was sent to Pennsylvania, where his father had bought land. In 1805 Audubon completed his first series of bird sketches. After several other career changes,

by 1821 he was still producing illustrations of birds but without much commercial success. He finally completed the Birds of America series in 1837. It was an enormous work, consisting of 435 plates, each bird depicted both life size and in its natural environment. He also wrote about the birds' habits and his own experiences of life traveling across America. He then embarked on an illustrated series of animals of America, which took him again through the United States, including the South, where to earn money he acted as a tutor. With the success of the Birds of America series giving him financial security, he moved with his family to Louisiana and Philadelphia, before finally settling in New York City, where he died in 1851.

André-Charles Boulle

ANDRÉ-CHARLES BOULLE (1642–1732) was a French cabinetmaker who specialized in making intricately designed furniture, often characterized by its inlaid marquetry of tortoiseshell, brass, and ivory. He was the most celebrated of Louis XIV's furniture makers, and his work was prized for its delicacy and inventiveness. After he died, his workshop continued to produce beautiful objects, and Boulle-style clock cases, bureaus, and commodes were greatly treasured. The Boulle technique of using an inlay of ebony or mahogany, with precious woods, mother-of-pearl, gilded brass, and, later, copper remains unique in the history of inlaid furniture.

George Peter Alexander Healy

G. P. A. HEALY (1813–1894) was a protégé of Thomas Sully and studied painting in Paris, where he received an important commission from King Louis-Philippe of France to paint a series of portraits of famous Americans for the palace of Versailles. Healy returned to America and settled in Chicago from 1855 to 1865. Inspired by the Civil War generals, he traveled south and painted portraits of Ulysses S. Grant, William T. Sherman, George B. McClellan, and other Southern dignitaries. Perhaps never as famous as Sully, he nonetheless had a successful career and died in 1894.

Prudent Francis Mallard

PRUDENT FRANCIS MALLARD was born in 1809 in Sèvres, France. He became a cabinetmaker and immigrated to New York in 1829. He worked there until 1838, when he moved to New Orleans and opened a workshop on Royal Street. His furniture became enormously successful, his designs in the Rococo Revival and Renaissance styles feeding the fashion of the time for Southern plantation house interiors. He often used exotic woods from South and Central America, and as well as providing hundreds of pieces for Southern patrons, he also exported his work to Europe. He died in 1879 and is buried in Metairie Cemetery, New Orleans.

William H. Ranlett

WILLIAM H. RANLETT (1806–1865) was a hugely influential American architect and author during the mid-nineteenth century. His journal, *The Architect,* which started publication in 1846, was the most important contribution to American architecture at the time. In it, Ranlett drew designs for houses, with floor plans and elevations, listing materials and prices (from nine hundred to twelve thousand dollars) in such a way that both architects and clients could choose a style and formulate a budget. The designs were very wide ranging, offering clients a choice of Elizabethan, Grecian, Gothic, Swiss, Indian, French, and Anglo-Italian. Other architects, such as Samuel Sloan, also published their designs in book form, but Ranlett's was by far the most popular, and his catalogs directed the progress of residential architecture throughout the nineteenth century.

Samuel Sloan

SAMUEL SLOAN IS one of the best-known American architects of the mid-nineteenth century. Born in Pennsylvania in 1815, Sloan spent most of his life in Philadelphia, honing his architectural skills by mostly working on institutions such as the state penitentiary and local hospitals. Later he began to excel at designing private residences, favoring the Italianate style that had become very popular by the 1840s. After some financial setbacks, later in his career he worked mostly in North Carolina, designing a state asylum and many private residences throughout the Carolinas and Alabama. He died in Raleigh in 1884.

INDEX

Page numbers in *italics* indicate illustration captions.